THE POWER OF YIN
CELEBRATING FEMALE CONSCIOUSNESS

THE POWER OF YIN
CELEBRATING FEMALE CONSCIOUSNESS

BY HAZEL HENDERSON,
JEAN HOUSTON, AND
BARBARA MARX HUBBARD

EDITED BY BARBARA DELANEY

PHOTOS BY MARY CLARE POWELL

COSIMO

NEW YORK

The resources are going to run out in fifty years! Why do you suppose people like ourselves are trying to find these alternate modes of being, and to tap the enormous ecology of inner space? The ecological holocaust is twofold: it has to do with the gross overuse of our external environment, and the incredible underuse of internal environment.

——Jean Houston, speaking in 1977, in *The Power of Yin*

*When Yang has reached its greatest strength,
the dark power of Yin is born within its depths...*
—The I Ching

The Power of Yin! A celebration of the
female principle. An informal exploration
of the female sensibility and its responses
to the challenge of a world environment
seriously threatened by the excesses
of masculine—*Yang*—ways of
being and behaving.

THE POWER OF YIN

CELEBRATING FEMALE CONSCIOUSNESS

BY HAZEL HENDERSON,
JEAN HOUSTON, AND
BARBARA MARX HUBBARD

EDITED BY BARBARA DELANEY

PHOTOS BY MARY CLARE POWELL

TABLE OF CONTENTS

THE VIEW FROM 2006
by Hazel Henderson

August 2006

I found the thirty-year-old manuscript of this book in one of my overlooked files in 2005. Somehow it had survived my move from Princeton, New Jersey, in the late 1970s to Gainesville, Florida, home of the University of Florida, and finally to St. Augustine, where I have lived for the past twenty years. As I reread the manuscript, masterfully edited by Barbara DeLaney and based on hours of audiotapes recorded during a marathon meeting of minds over two weekends in 1977 and 1978, I was struck with how the many topics and issues covered in these conversations seemed timeless, even current.

Human life spans are almost irrelevant to many of the topics I and my dear friends Jean Houston and Barbara Marx Hubbard addressed in the wide-ranging conversations reproduced in this book, and continue to address in our work. We don't look for short-term outcomes or surface ripples on the mighty river of human history. We are concerned with deep currents below the surface, processes of social change that are beyond the span of one or several lifetimes. Mahatma Gandhi was once asked about the effects of the French Revolution. His answer: "It's too early to tell."

In this age of instant gratification, 24/7 electronic news—all in soundbites—we miss both the slow-motion good news and bad news. Slow-motion good news I have been tracking all my adult life is the great transition from fossil-fueled industrialism to the cleaner, greener renewable energy and resources of what I call the Solar Age. Barely visible in the 1970s, these new technologies designed with Nature in mind: organic agriculture, preventive health care, and solar, wind, and ocean power are now growing at double-digit rates worldwide. By 2005, it was possible for me to create a TV series, *Ethical Markets*, to document this growing "green" economy worldwide and see it aired by PBS stations covering 45 million households. Some of the slow-motion bad news that worried me in the 1970s, when I was serving on the Advisory Council to the U.S. Office of Technology Assessment, was global warming, evident even back then. This issue has also emerged into the mainstream—along with global concerns about clean drinking water, rising sea levels, loss of biodiversity, and desertification—none too soon.

The issues that are still on the human agenda that threaten our survival concern our own cognitive, emotional, and spiritual evolution. Our technological prowess has now created human interdependence and the globalization out of our formerly disparate futures. Yet the historical mind-sets that ensured us survival to this point—territoriality, competition for resources, self-interest separateness, materialism, fears of scarcity and each other, and our vulnerability to the forces of nature—will surely destroy us. All these ancient mind-sets still form the core theories about human nature in our prevailing economic models. Thus, a large part of my writing and speaking over the past thirty years has been to expose the economics of our reptilian brains: a malfunctioning economic source code deep in the hard drives of all our institutions and cultural belief systems.

Thus, the next chapter of the human agendas requires nothing less than the evolution of our own awareness and consciousness. Only in this way can we overcome violence and conflict and reintegrate human knowledge and the explosion of brilliance during our period of Cartesian exploration and experimentation. Slow-motion good news on this emerging new human is hard to find in our mass media, with its commercial formulas of covering rape, riot, and ruin: "if it bleeds it leads." Likewise, mainstream financial media has managed to overlook or ridicule ethical investing, corporate social responsibility, and the growing "green" sectors of the global economy.

I have been committed to the processes of human evolution and social development, and it is these passionate pursuits that brought me into continuous closeness and deep companionship with my beloved sisters, Jean Houston and Barbara Marx Hubbard. They, too, have their own thoughts on the changes wrought by the thirty years since our intellectual summit meeting, and the human family's prospects for a common planetary future.

JEAN HOUSTON'S STATEMENT

When Hazel Henderson informed me that the manuscript of *The Power of Yin* would be published, I could only laugh. For laughter is largely what I remember from those golden autumn days of 1977 when Barbara Marx Hubbard and I sat together with Hazel in her lovely Princeton home and spoke together of our hopes and dreams of making a better world through the power of yin. I thought that a transcription of the tapes of a similar meeting in April 1978 would yield page after page of "Ha ha ha ha ha ha ha!"

Viewing this material now from the vista of thirty years later, I am stunned at how prescient were our conversations of so long ago. And also, how much of our current lives are fractals of what we envisioned then. Here I am, still teaching a school of spiritual and psychological studies, but now amplified into many programs in social artistry for leaders the world over. Hazel's and Barbara's work has reached so many people and arenas worldwide that truly they can be said to be among those who have profoundly made a difference to this world and time. And strangely (or foolishly), age does not seem to wither nor custom stale our continued efforts to improve the planetary and human condition. The power of yin moves among us, between us, within us, as well it should, for without it, the human experiment could well come to an ending in the next hundred years or so. Where is this yin power leading us?

I sometimes attend conferences of high-minded folk from many disciplines who address the problems of an old world passing into a new. The millennium has brought many to the table. Some are radical visionaries proposing utopian global housecleanings. Others are reformers devoted to redressing old wrongs. Each attempts to push the membrane that wraps us in unknowing. With all their practical skill and accomplishments, they are humble before the mystery of a world in transition.

"It is as if we are in a giant womb, trying to figure out what happens next," a United Nations official said to me recently at the State of the World Forum.

I was startled by her remark, for earlier that day, I had been chatting about international politics with a Bulgarian cab driver in San Francisco. "I have just been present at the birth of my daughter," he told me. "I was very afraid, for I had never seen such a thing. It was very messy and very beautiful. And after all the hours of my wife's labor and the painful contractions, a new life! Maybe that is what is trying to happen in our world."

Like Hazel and Barbara, I sometimes think of my work as a kind of midwifery. Organizations and cultures, businesses, as well as individuals, sometimes need a steadying hand as they birth themselves into a world as strange and unexpected as the one babies face when they emerge from the womb.

But how do we do it? How do we grow to become stewards of the extraordinary time that is upon us, and it so doing nurture ourselves, our clients, even our various cultures? One way is realizing the extent of the whole-system transition of which we are a part—a condition of interactive change that affects every aspect of life as we know it. I call it Jump Time. It is related to what in evolutionary biology is called punctuated equilibrium. Change, evolutionary theorists tell us, doesn't happen gradually. Rather, things go along as they were for a long while—in a state of equilibrium—until a species, living at the edge of its tolerance, experiences enough ferment and stress to punctuate the equilibrium with a sudden jump to a whole new order of being.

It is the changing of the guard on every level, in which every given is quite literally up for grabs. It is the momentum behind the drama of the world, the breakdown and breakthrough of every old way of being, knowing, relating, governing, and believing. It shakes the foundations of all and everything. And sometimes, it even allows for another order of reality to come into time. Throughout history there have been many cultural jumps, but what is looming before us now is a collective jump—faster and more complex than any the world has known. We find ourselves at present in the midst of the most massive shift of perspective humankind has ever known. Other times thought they were it. They were wrong. This is it.

In a Jump Time, with everything in transition, we can no longer afford to live as remedial members of the human race. A new set of values—holistic, syncretic, relationship- and process-oriented, organic, spiritual—is rising within us and around us. These, of course, are women's values, women's genius, women's gift. These are the powers of yin!

Though old forces and traditions and fears seek to restrain us, we know there is no going back. Our complex time requires a wiser use of our capacities, a richer music from the instrument we have been given. The world will thrive only if we can grow. The possible society will become a reality only if we learn to be the possible humans we are capable of being. As women, we are the pilgrims and the parents of this new emerging world, and no old formulas and stopgap solutions will do. In the past, men in governments and the private sector have been partners in determining how the world works. It is time now to focus on the role that women—who are the majority of the people on the Earth, a majority that has been largely excluded in the past—should play in the development process. This is indispensable if we seek a future that is different from the past.

Women are critical to the great forces of change: the repatterning of human nature, the regenesis of human society, the breakdown of the membrane between cultures and peoples, the breakthrough of the depths, both psychological and spiritual. And so the rise of women in our time and in the century before us may be one of the most important happenings in human history.

BARBARA MARX HUBBARD'S STATEMENT

How things have changed in thirty years!

This is a whole generation that we have lived as three sisters in deep engagement with the work of evolving our selves and our society. It feels so close, so present, almost a collapse of time.

In rereading the manuscript I was first of all struck by how coherent it was. I had, as Jean said, memories of a great deal of laughter and friendship. But now I see that we actually were even then seeded with the creative impulse that we each have manifested in the last three decades. We are carriers of "templates" of evolutionary design codes of the emerging human world.

It feels to me as though Jean, Hazel, and myself—along with countless others—are mothering a new world, literally giving it birth by giving our creative lives for its manifestation. In this giving we are deeply rewarded, for we are, through this continuous expression, evolving ourselves into the new humans that we are envisioning and supporting for others. In other words, by giving our gifts we are learning to model and be the change we want to see in the world.

My greatest blessing has been this sense of prime vocation, an innate calling or soul's code that motivates me to give and express purpose as best I can.

I can see that my two friends felt I was "under the thumb of men" at that time. The fact is that I had never met women who truly inspired me until I met Jean and Hazel. Everyone who had influenced me—Teilhard de Chardin, Sri Aurobindo, Buckminster Fuller, Abraham Maslow, Jonas Salk, and many more—were men. All my creative partners were men. Now of course, I know many remarkable women and work with them, but at the time of the time of our conversation, that had not happened. And on intimate level, after eighteen years with my partner, Sidney Lanier, we have finally learned what we call coequal cocreative partnership. Even though I was a liberated woman in many ways in the 70s, the cultural imprint of feeling that a man would know best was so deep that it has taken a whole lifetime to free myself of that.

On the social front, it seems to me that what we said then has only intensified and become more apparent in these last thirty years, and therefore, we are more called out into the work than ever before.

The breakdown of current social systems and dominant patriarchal structure is more obvious. There is a desperate last-ditch stand of the old power structure to maintain itself. The flaws in the system are more apparent; the violence born of oppression, inequality, and regressive memes are closer to the surface. The failure of war to win anything is becoming clearer. And there is a new uprising of revulsion against war as a way of deciding anything. The failure of unlimited, competitive commercial growth is now obvious as we discover its destruction of community and environment, and its failure to nourish the human spirit. The systemic breakdown of the environment is far more obvious than it was when we met. The threat to our life-support systems is now front-page news.

The time frame for change has shortened. The "macroshift" or bifurcation point where the system either breaks down or breaks through to a higher, more synergistic order is very close, many of us feel. Concurrently with these obvious breakdowns, there has been a rapid acceleration of breakthroughs, of innovations in every field and function. The global civil society is arising as the most potent force on Earth. We have reached "critical mess." A perfect crisis! It cannot be resolved by doing more of the same.

We are at the stage in the movement for conscious evolution where the nonlinear, exponential interaction of innovating elements is ready to happen. Many networks of networks are now forming, learning to interact with one another as organic new functions in health, education, economics, media, and other arenas. The new social body is taking shape right now, in our midst. It is truly the most exiting time to be alive.

Jean, Hazel, and I are among the many women throughout the world who are now manifesting what I think of as a new feminine archetype: the feminine cocreator. Standing on the shoulder of our sisters who paved the way, we are women who are motivated from within by a process of creativity, a prime vocation that feels as though it comes from the larger design of evolution. It expresses itself in loving action not to be equal to men in a dysfunctional world but to cocreate a new world equal to our spiritual, social, and scientific and technological capacities.

Evolutionary women are on the rise. And we seem to create a new context in which evolutionary men are freer to release themselves from the bonds of patriarchy and join together in new forms of real partnership. We are giving birth to a new human and a new humanity within ourselves. This universal human is connected through the heart to the whole of life, is awakened from within by the desire to create and participate, is expanding toward a more multidimensional consciousness and creativity, and is literally transcending the self-conscious, limited phase of Homo *sapiens sapiens.*

I am doing many wonderful projects with partners throughout the country and world, among them a DVD series called *Humanity Ascending: A New Way through Together.* I offer the new worldview of conscious evolution as an explorer on the evolutionary edge. The series is designed to reach as many people as possible, to awaken in people their evolutionary code of self and social evolution. I am in the process of cocreating a "communion of pioneering souls," who feel this emergence within them. It is a most precious global community upon this Earth, from every race, nation, and religion connected in a morphic or resonant field by attunement to what is emerging within ourselves and the world.

At 76 I am deep into "regenopause." This is, I believe a new life cycle in the life of a woman. When we enter menopause, and are no longer producing eggs—we ourselves are the "egg." It is our time to give birth the authentic feminine self and our work in the world. As we have fewer children and live longer lives, this feminine cocreator is arising with up to fifty years of lifetime ahead of her. The evolutionary regenopausal woman is a guide to the younger women as well as to men. She heralds the future of our species and as far as I can tell is the critical community of guidance and leadership to carry us through his transition toward a universal humanity.

*　　*　　*

All three of us—Jean, Barbara, and myself hope you will find these conversations a peek into our deeply personal sharing of our highest aspirations. We are all profoundly grateful to Barbara DeLaney—a young student at the time, but wise beyond her years—for her dedicated work in turning hundreds of audiotapes into such a coherent book. We invited Barbara to add her final thoughts.

BARBARA DELANEY'S STATEMENT

When Hazel telephoned earlier this year to ask if I still had a decent copy of our old manuscript, I went immediately to the attic. I couldn't find the manuscript, but did come across my old IBM Selectric II electric typewriter—the very one I had used, in my Boswellian role, to work and rework *The Power of Yin*. It had been at that time quite cutting-edge, with its font-changing, pivoting textball and self-correcting tape. Who could have imagined anything more ultramodern? And there it was, nearly thirty years later, a neglected relic. This was exactly my concern for our dusty manuscript: would it, too, be a mere artifact of a different time and place?

I was finally able to reread *The Power of Yin* when a scanned copy of the original manuscript (my original typos and all) was e-mailed to me. Rereading the old manuscript on my Dell color monitor, I was surprised and very excited to find that the text seemed remarkably fresh and timely, its themes compellingly relevant to our new century and its relentlessly threatening challenges.

I write this at a time that seems increasingly fraught with impending catastrophe. It is apparent that we as a country, and indeed, as a planetary civilization, may be nearing the point of no return. We are exhausting our resources while facing potential ecological collapse as a result of our waste-producing technologies. Social and racial inequalities are increasing at a perilous rate, thanks in no small part to an administration interested only in the short-term well-being of its admitted constituency of the "haves and have mores," while our country engages in disastrous, unprovoked war. Nuclear proliferation remains an ever-increasing danger. As the bumper sticker on my Prius—you can't know Hazel Henderson and drive an SUV—reads: "If you aren't completely appalled, you haven't been paying attention."

Without a full-scale change in orientation, it is hard to imagine that we might avoid, at best, a slide into the chaos and social disruption of continuous low-grade ecological disaster, or, at worst, a catastrophic annihilation of life as we know it. We are witnessing the inevitable outcomes of the testosterone-fueled yang belief systems of the dominant male culture—consequences prophetically warned against in the pages of *The Power of Yin.* Clearly, there is now more than ever a desperate need for a radically different kind of vision to inform the choices that we, as a planetary civilization, are facing. I was convinced some thirty years ago, and am now yet more adamantly convinced, that the three amazing women you will come to know in these pages present different yet vital aspects of a positive, radically transformative vision of how we might evolve as women and as men in the twenty-first century.

It's no longer politically incorrect to talk about gender differences; indeed, a recently published book—*The Female Brain,* by Dr. Luann Brizendine—clearly delineates the hormonally primed divergence in brain architecture and chemistry between women and men; it seems that evolution *has* hardwired us to think differently. But the discourse never seems to progress much beyond how those differences play out from the sandbox to the workplace, in education, and in relationships. The much larger idea of a world reimagined—reconceived!—as an expression of female-engendered values, belief systems, and organizational structures, the pivotal theme of *The Power of Yin,* is an idea whose time has finally come. An idea not revolutionary, but evolutionary.

On a more personal level, the last few decades have taken me on a path through motherhood, a period of antinuclear activism (inspired by Hazel and her many years of environmental activism), and various artistic endeavors, including dance, a continuing career as a teacher of competitive figure skating, and, more recently, oil painting. My nest newly empty, I am now at the threshold of a new stage in my life. I remember Jean Houston talking about Margaret Mead and her idea of the power of "postmenopausal zest." It then seemed impossibly far off, but time has a way moving us forward, and I am now at a point of zestful self-reinvention. What better time to have rediscovered the female wisdom so wonderfully expressed in *The Power of Yin,* and to find it as deeply inspiring today as it was in 1977.

My profound thanks, once again, to Hazel, Jean, and Barbara, all as awe-inspiring as ever.

INTRODUCTION

This book is the outcome of an extraordinary convergence of three remarkable female minds. The pure exhilaration I am left with, having had the extreme good fortune to have witnessed this encounter, empowers me to attempt to record—and thereby to share—this profound affirmation of a different kind of feminism. Finally! At a time when most are committed to minimizing the distinction between male and female consciousness, here are women who dare to be *other* than men; to admit, without qualification, that *we are different*!

It's a great awakening—the emergence of a new kind of woman from behind the veil of traditionally imposed conditionings and role encapsulations. Active, intelligent, strongly committed women who are evolving a new consciousness of the potentialities of female beingness, and who are beginning to apply that consciousness to larger issues, to realms historically dominated by male thinking and masculine images and values. That dominion is being challenged. Sometimes quietly; sometimes with great éclat. To those who would question this, I offer *The Power of Yin* as an introduction to the power and resources of feminine consciousness.

The women participating in the conversations transcribed in this book are all representative of this new breed of women. Together they form a fascinating triad of perspectives; a communion of highly evolved sensibilities, each one illuminating unique, but complementary aspects of a different kind of vision. A distinctly *feminine* vision. There is tremendous energy in their dialogue; a strong sense of solidarity with one another, and with all of us who are committed to evolving as women, and as human beings.

We live in a time of transition. Female identity, as we all know, is still a confused issue. We have outgrown the old images, but the new ones aren't yet clear. And so we need to explore new kinds of roles and images. Such is my purpose in presenting these dialogues. This is a book about images. Alternatives. Possibilities. About women at various stages of personal evolution attempting to define the parameters of their own growth and transformation. Although differing in approach and focus, these women are all social transformers commonly bonded by an active commitment to evolutionary change, to radical new visions of human possibility.

*　*　*

It was through Hazel Henderson that I first met Jean Houston and Barbara Hubbard in 1976 while spending some time with Hazel at her home in Princeton. Hazel had been very excited at the prospect of an informal meeting with Barbara and Jean, and suggested that perhaps I, too, as a young woman, might be interested in what was to be the focus of that meeting: feminine consciousness. Would I like to make tape recordings of those conversations? It was an intriguing offer, of course, and I accepted with great anticipation—but having no notion of what was to transpire, or of how it was to alter some basic premises I had and dramatically confirm others.

Hazel Henderson, for those not familiar with her widely acknowledged thinking and far-reaching activities, has become over the past decade one of the most enlightened and *enlightening* public activists of our time. Being virtually self-educated—and thus free from much of the systematic intellectual programming to which most of us are subjected—and never having defined herself in terms of any one discipline, Hazel has the ability to extract the common elements from a wide variety of disciplines, to determine what is valuable, and to synthesize those elements into a highly innovative genre of economic and social thinking that transcends conventional, reductionistic intellectual habits. She reveals the cultural myopia that prevents the dominant powers from seeing that, indeed, the resources *are* running out; that the old systems and values are rapidly becoming dysfunctional; that viable countereconomies and lifestyles are already burgeoning into being. As evidenced in these dialogues, Hazel has preserved a mode of thinking uncorrupted by prevailing masculine biases, and a purity of vision strongly resistant to the omnipresent pressure of masculine standards. At a time of widespread moral and ethical bankruptcy, here is a voice that resounds with a rare intellectual integrity.

Hazel is an eloquent, commanding woman who exudes vitality, warmth, a sense of fun, and *joie de vivre*. She speaks with vigor, clarity, a vocabulary at once earthy and elegant. Hazel *lives* the values she so fervently espouses; this, beyond all else, is what makes her so deeply inspiring to those of us who have come to know and love her. Hazel *is* all that she wants us to be.

Jean Houston is a dramatic presence with a mane of dark hair and a full, exuberant laughter that seems to emanate from the solar plexus; a woman of incredible energy and an unusual intensity of mind and spirit. At that first meeting in Princeton, I was somewhat stunned, admittedly, by her breathtaking command of language and prodigious store of knowledge and ideas. But Jean's gifts, as I quickly discovered, are not merely intellectual. Her activities and achievements span an amazing range, but she is best known for her pioneering work in the field of human potential.

Later, Jean invited me to participate in one of the many intensive workshops she conducts at the Dromenon Center for Change, based on her years of research as codirector of the Foundation for Mind Research in Pomona, New York. Dromenon—like Jean herself!—is a remarkable experience. During her workshops she functions as a kind of priestess, initiating participants into whole new modes of learning, of experiencing—of *being*. She invokes a wide variety of techniques—from the ancient and exotic to advanced psychophysical exercises—to induce awareness of mind/body capacities either long forgotten by our culture, or perhaps not yet evolved. One emerges with an enlarged conception of one's own capacities and a dynamic new image of human evolutionary potential.

Jean brings to every encounter a very deep, very human interest; she listens with absorption, seems to respond with her whole being, is full of questions (rarely *Why?*, most frequently *Why not?*), challenges, provocative insights. She is by profession both teacher and therapist; her heuristic approach is pivotal to many of the dialogues that follow.

The third voice in these fascinating trilogues is Barbara Marx Hubbard, an uncommonly sensitive intelligence. A visionary. A woman whose personal quest for meaning has evolved into what might be described as an almost religious vision of the evolutionary transformation of humankind. While many have begun to conceptualize the image of an imminent planetary society, Barbara's vision is more cosmic in scope—humanity as one body emerging into the cosmos as a universal species.

One cannot but be deeply impressed with Barbara's unique sense of role and purpose: her fervent dedication to the task of communicating *positive* images of the future—a future of unlimited possibility. As cofounder of the Washington, D.C.–based Committee for the Future, she has become a leading "evolutionary futurist"; she is well known for her efforts to stimulate popular support for space exploration programs, and for her promotion of an imaginative technique of group problem-solving she calls SYNCON (Synergistic Convergence). SYNCON, like all of Barbara's activities, is an attempt to make connections, to coordinate, to fuse—an orchestration of evolutionary images and networks of evolutionary beings.

Barbara is a luminous, captivating personality, a woman deeply in touch with her inner being. She speaks expansively, with disarming candor and honesty. At the time of these conversations, she had come with a strong need for support, sharing—for *communion*—and frequently becomes the focus of conversations probing deep inner needs and meanings. It was, in fact, Barbara who had arranged this meeting in Princeton. In a letter she recalled for me the exchange that had inspired her to do so:

I had sent Jean Houston a copy of my book, The Hunger of Eve, *and happened to call her several weeks later. She announced to me in her dramatic way that my life had "recapitulated the historic transformation" and that I was about to "embody the next stage of history"!*

Naturally, I was intrigued and questioned her.

"Barbara, your life has paralleled the great periods of history—the Neolithic nurturing and caring; the Mesolithic period of helping men structure large systems... And now you and our civilization are entering a new phase. You may be the first

to make the transformation in one lifetime."

I told her I felt on the brink of a consciousness breakthrough… as though a cosmic fetus were about to hatch in my head.

She then asked whether I identified with Jesus or St. Paul. After the initial shock of the question, I answered, St. Paul. I had been struck by a powerfully motivating awareness ten years ago: that humankind was being born into the universe; that our age is the transition from Earth-only to universal life, literally. I had received an inner commandment: "Go tell the story of the birth of humankind." I had been working to fulfill that commandment ever since. I identified with St. Paul in the sense of trying to share the good news.

"But you must stop identifying with Paul and start identifying with Jesus!" she proclaimed. "Women must become primary channels of godfulness."

"Are you talking about feminine consciousness?" I asked.

"Yes!"

"Well, what exactly is feminine consciousness?"

She began to expound upon this theme and I interrupted her suddenly. "Jean, I feel the need to talk about this in depth with you—to explore this stage of consciousness at leisure. Maybe just you and I… or maybe with someone else, too. How about Hazel Henderson? She's the other most powerful woman I know, besides you. She's very different—an environmentalist, a brilliant economist; she's the terror of multinational corporations. She disagrees with me about the vital importance of the space program, but I love her, and she loves me. Perhaps among us we could understand what it is that we're going through.

I called Hazel and she immediately agreed to meet. The date was set for January 17, 1977, at Hazel's home in Princeton, New Jersey.

The Henderson home is an older, rambling house full of inviting corners, intriguing books, plants, sunny spaces. When everyone had arrived on that icy January day, we gathered cozily in the living room amongst discretely placed tape recorders.

The conversation that day immediately seemed to assume a will of its own. We would agree to limit all discussion to "trivia" for the duration of a lunch or dinner break, but even trivia would lead irresistibly to some terribly provocative topic other, and I would be dispatched—*Hold the thought!*—to find a tape recorder. And so many of these conversations were actually recorded over bread, cheese, and wine in the dining room, the clatter of dishes in the kitchen, and even over "Aunt Hazel's" homemade granola at breakfast.

I have tried to recreate this meeting, which lasted until the evening of the following day, in the form of a collection of dialogues transcribed from the tapes made at that time. I have chosen the dialogue form in an attempt to preserve the spontaneous and informal quality of the experience, and to evoke a sense of the rich and dynamic interplay of feelings and ideas. This form, however, was in at least one way problematic: the dialogue is often intensely animated, joyous; it is frequently punctuated with peals of ebullient laughter—how does one transcribe laughter?

My method has been one of selective editing. I have tried to eliminate redundancies without disrupting the natural flow and have occasionally eliminated an entire conversation if it seemed in some way inappropriate or not of general interest. Where necessary I have slightly paraphrased or rearranged things in order to make a more concise statement, but without being in any way unfaithful to the substance of the original thought or choice of words.

Although the conversations encompass a broad range of themes and an interesting juxtaposition of perspectives, the central proposition comes through clearly—that the minds of women differ from the minds of men! Where not explicit, this distinction is nonetheless manifest on several levels—in the *method* of exploring ideas as well as in the points of view. The result is an abundance of themes filtered through the alembic of the female sensibility.

I was impressed immediately, in listening to these women, with the way in which they were able to move so easily from the objective to the subjective, and back again to the objective. I couldn't help imagining a parallel scenario: three male intellectual "heavyweights" gathered for the express purpose of discussing, say, masculine consciousness. One would expect such dialogues to be, I dare suggest, rigorously objective, impersonal, abstracted.

I was both relieved and excited to find something very different happening here. Although rich in intellectual content, the dialogues function primarily as the vehicle for a penetrating process of mutual self-exploration. This becomes a means of unveiling some of the essential qualities of female experience as it relates to the forging of new roles and images. Throughout the conversations, regardless of the subject at hand, there is a deep sense of personal significance—through exploring the personal, the transpersonal meaning is brought into focus. There is no fear of exposure: these are women who dare to be vulnerable; to express the inner sources of their motivations, their pain, their uncertainties—and, indeed, their strengths. The kind of thinking that takes place is a wonderful manifestation of "yin" thinking: there is an integration of the feeling and intuitive functions with rational, objective faculties; a healthy mix of earthy female body wisdom and forceful intellectual clarity.

"Yin" thinking, to use the Chinese symbolism, is by no means accessible only to women; it is central to the New Age consciousness evolving in both women and men. The terms *masculine* and *feminine*, or *yang* and *yin*, are useful ways of describing, by way of metaphor, two distinct but complementary modes of consciousness and a complex of mutually defining qualities—analysis/synthesis, rational/intuitive, object/subject, and so on. Western culture has for centuries been strongly overbalanced in favor of the so-called "masculine" principles. We are taught at an early age to cultivate linear, analytic, dichotomizing patterns of thinking at the expense of the more diffused, intuitive, holistic "yin" patterns. Women, having a broader range of experiential knowledge and less rigidly defined intellectual commitments, seem to be more attuned than men, at this point in time, to these other worldviews. As the chief bearers of feminine attributes, we as women have a critical role to play in the transformation of our masculine culture into a more balanced, more *human* order.

In these dialogues the yin/yang distinction is perhaps most vividly exposed in terms of value considerations. It is becoming ever more apparent that many of the primary values woven into our cultural fabric are strongly linked to what have been deemed "masculine" traits of character. The consequences of such ingrained habits as competition, material growth at any cost, and social and environmental dominance and control are becoming manifest in the form of diminishing natural resources, serious ecological disruptions, and increasingly unmanageable social inequities and injustices. Not to mention the threat of thermonuclear power games—the ultimate manifestation of excessive "virility." The human species is faced with a critical challenge: Can we achieve a new orientation of consciousness embracing values traditionally disparaged as "feminine"?

But what exactly *is* a feminine orientation of consciousness? As so beautifully illuminated in these dialogues, it is an essentially humanistic consciousness emerging from the feminine tendency to cherish, to nourish, to preserve. Not Man as Conqueror, but Woman as Nurturer. No longer inexorably bonded to reproductive functions, the emerging new woman is increasingly turning her female energies to the much larger tasks of nurturing the species and preserving our threatened life-support system. This implies a different kind of creativity—a holistic creativity sensitive, above all, to the requirements of life-oriented growth and process.

Female thinking and social wisdom reflects a whole complex of new forms and conceptualizations. It is a thinking that is *qualitative* rather than quantitative: growth, for example, is seen not in terms of gross national product, but in terms of the unlimited growth potential of *human* resources. It is characterized by an aversion to hierarchies—an artifact of patriarchal structuring—and an instinctive tendency toward more flexible networking forms. Women have a deep sense of the cooperative, sharing ways that will be essential to our survival as an interdependent planetary species.

The reemergence in Western culture of yin values and psychological faculties may, indeed, be a kind of innate survival response to conditions produced by the excesses of yang. This is not to suggest that the yin might be superior to the yang—is night better than day, light more useful than dark? Both are essential—one-sidedness in either direction would be counterproductive. The object is rather a reintegration of opposing energies; a creative interplay of the intellectual and the intuitive, the objective and the subjective, the logical and the imaginative. Rational-scientific thinking infused with subjective value considerations and intuitive insight is a thinking of a much higher order. In the ancient Taoist vision, the universe is seen as a rhythmic fluctuation of masculine and feminine energies, each in its abundance initiating the other—a continuous process of change engendered by a dynamic equilibrium of yin and yang. The cultivation of creative dialogue between the masculine and feminine will be a profound enrichment of our cultural mind-set.

As a woman, I am deeply affected by the peculiarly feminine vision that emerges from these dialogues. The women of my generation are beginning to experience the positive effects of changes accomplished through the efforts of the feminist movement; we need no longer be obsessed *merely* with the struggle to improve our status as human beings. We are beginning to explore the myriad possibilities of female beingness, to define ourselves in new and authentically female ways, to devise our own calculus of human value. The endeavor to achieve sexual parity does not mean recreating ourselves in the image *man*: We must allow ourselves to think as women, to act as women, to commit ourselves *as women*. It is only through the uninhibited celebration of our femaleness that we can hope to realize the full potential of what we as women have to contribute to the next stage of human evolution.

We offer these dialogues not only for the value of the ideas and insights they contain, but also, and most important, in hope of generating more dialogue, more evolutionary exploration, more genuinely yin thinking.

Barbara DeLaney
1978

I

"How Do You Find a Paradigm for an Emergent?"

*Eros and Logos. The rising of the depths.
The critical density of global interdependence:
a flowering of world civilization. The overendowment
of human brain capacity. Self-educated women: no
intellectual investment. The synergizing Earth,
Cosmic consciousness, and the universal species.*

*Monday morning, January 17, 1977. The following
conversation, though tending to be more monologue
than dialogue, sets the tone and establishes themes
from which later dialogues flow.*

Barbara: Okay, ladies. I think I've got this all together. We're on tape now.

Jean: First of all—Barbara, how are you? I haven't had a chance to ask.

Barbara: Good. I'm as good as I can be at this stage of my life.

Jean: Meaning . . .? Are you not feeling well?

Barbara: I'm feeling fine. Physically I'm fine. It's mentally that I'm not sure about! *[laughter]*

Jean: No, but you do look a little harried. Are you?

Barbara: Yes. I am, as a matter of fact.

Jean: You have to watch that or you'll come down with a lovely illness of one sort or another.

Hazel: *(setting down a tray with four cups of tea)* That's right. I think that's something we all have to watch out for with the kinds of lives we all lead . . . Will you all help yourselves to milk and honey?

Barbara: Oh, that's lovely, Hazel. So let's begin, then, at the beginning. We're all here right now because of some things that Jean had said to me the last time we talked, which has been several months now. You were talking, Jean, about feminine consciousness, and the fact that it has gone through three major transformations. Why don't you state this thesis, and then we might talk about where we are, and what this new form of consciousness might become.

Jean: I was actually looking at three major periods of history. Civilization begins with the Neolithic period, when man stops depending upon the meanderings of the hunt and begins to settle down into agricultural societies. These, of course, were the great Neolithic societies, most of which were dominated by matrilinear forms. Women did not govern, but there was much more creative interplay between male and female elements in the society. The great goddess cults evolved from this. The impetus here is one of tribal interdependence and very intense organization in which each part is related to every other part. The thrust principle would be Eros as opposed to Logos. I don't mean Eros in terms of sexuality, but Eros in terms of the fine symbiotic connections between things—essentially the love principle.

With the coming of the great city-states, especially along the Tigris-Euphrates Valley, came the urban revolutions that were always male-dominated. Instead of a seamless web of kinship, as in the Neolithic societies, they were based on hierarchical, highly structured typologies and very specific kinds of functions—a division of the human into parts. You inevitably have rather exclusive male dominance in these societies, with females being relegated to functions and functionaries. The thrust here is Logos: linear chains of being.

Somewhere around 500 B.C. we begin to see the breakdown of this. You have the rise of a lot of savior gods, especially between about 500 B.C. and the second or third century A.D., and a new kind of individuation. The great eras of mysticism occur at this time. The notion of a new kind of brotherhood begins to yeast here. Women are able to be participants in terms of spiritual realities, but not in terms of existential realities. You have also at the time the rise of major empire states—the Roman Empire, for example—which, again, are linear and hierarchical.

In our own time, with the extraordinary complexity of hierarchical events that you write about so well, Hazel, the hierarchical chain of being has begun to break down. With the breakdown of ontological structures—social, cosmic, moral, religious—there is a rising of the depths. When psychological energy is no longer bonded to social forms, it has to go elsewhere, and it goes inward. With this rising of the depths—which occurred also in the second-century Roman Empire, in seventeenth-century England with the coming of the Jacobean Era, and in Hitler's Germany—you have always the lowest common denominator: the soothsayers, the covens, the witches, the Gnostic sects. But also . . . there is the possibility of new forms of being. You see this with the Gnostic and Christian forms arising in the second century. It is a new kind of individuation in which there is really neither male nor female. It is a new combination of these in the human whole.

Normally we would probably have at this time the appearance of totalitarian leaders who will rise as Cromwell did, as some of the Roman emperors did, as Hitler did. They will rise in front of this ascendancy of rampant subjectivity and say: "I will give you peace! I will give you order! I will make things real again!" And the bliss-ninnies run into the first totalitarian embrace that comes along. As happened, for example, in Germany in the 1930s. After the Weimar Republic, after Berlin and the Bauhaus—which is the unconscious become flesh, after surrealism and the rising of the depths—you have the constrainments of a different kind of order. And it is generally an extremely demonic, masculine order in which the Logos has gone awry. The existential and sensory overloads, and the rising of the depths, are contained and constrained. It is forbidden to wear certain kinds of colors; the newspapers are restricted; brain function is politicized. For example, in the 1920s you have Mary Wigman's great dances and open movement; in Germany you have the new pattern of modern dance, the expression of subjectivity; and ten years later the national paradigm of movement and form is the goose step! In 1919 you have *The Cabinet of Dr. Caligari,* Euclidean nausea, angles falling away. And then, of course, in 1932, thirteen years later, you have the focusing of consciousness—hyperventilated consciousness: *Sieg Heil! Sieg Heil! Sieg Heil! Sieg Heil!*—on the charismatic, Logos-crazy leader. And look at what happens to architecture: Speer's plans for Germania, modern Peking . . .

Hazel: Mussolini . . .

Jean: Mussolini: *Il Duce! Il Duce! Il Duce!* . . . But I do not believe that this time we are going to fall into the totalitarian embrace. Not for reasons of science, but for reasons of history. The past two hundred years have witnessed the reclamation of human history on a large scale. We can see the historical cycles. We can see these patterns of rise and fall and thus begin to avoid the pattern of fatality.

In our time we have reached a critical density of global interdependence. There is such a resonance between the organism and the environment, ourselves and environment, environment and planet, and planet and god only knows what, that we are coming to a flowering of global civilization.

In my own work, for example, I do two types of things to find out about human potential. I take depth probings of the psyche. I will actually look intensely in many states of consciousness at what the capacities of any given individual are. I will also then take a cross-cultural approach. I look at the potentials throughout the inventories of human resources. Why is it that the Orunta have this acute orchestration of their senses? Why do the Eskimo think only in pictures? Why do the people of Uganda have this extraordinary plasticity and kinesthetic thinking through their hands? In this portrait we begin to get a portrait of the human condition and human capacities. It is a kind of implosion of human factors: a cross-cultural plurality of the givens of the human condition.

Suddenly for the first time in human history we have all left the cave! We have now entered into a coming global civilization, and with that is the quickening of the depths. This rising of the depths could mean global conflagration if we continue with the Logos principle laid down. Essentially what we had in Hitler and Il Duce and Stalin was the last stand of the city-state Logos typology. With the rising of the depths, and with the freedom of women from the encapsulation of roles, we are also witnessing the rise of feminine principles.

I have been putting people in trance for fifteen to twenty years now. I look at what is coming out. In the past five years or so there has been a radical change of imagery.

Barbara: In women?

Jean: In women and men. You never had a Wise Old Woman before; it was always the Wise Old Man. This is critical. The female principles are rising, not as Eros, but perhaps as Eros joined to Logos. Eros and Logos together in a new symbiosis is something else. Eros does not become what it becomes when it is isolated from Logos, which is sexuality to no purpose: *Playboy* magazine. It is Eros joined to Logos; in this new plurality and thickening, not only of global structure, but of ontological structure as well—inherent, depth structure. It becomes something very different: it becomes Eros as the mode of mediation of symbiosis between structures of events. Logos is the links, the building blocks, the sequencing that puts them together. Eros is the one that makes sure that it is organism-environment; that each structure is resonant in a quantum resonance to every other kind of structure. It is like a crystal in which each part yields many lights and refractions. This means that the feminine quality is rising in men, the masculine quality is rising in women, but it is not as simple as that. It is not the two put together; it is almost a new kind of gender and species. It is a different notion of what it means to be human.

In your economics, Hazel, this is essentially what you're doing. The metaphors are difficult because we have no paradigm for this. How do you find a paradigm for an emergent? This is the problem with so much of our work.

Hazel: Yes, exactly!

Jean: Paradigms are always *paradigmas* from the beginning! Ur! Archetypal! And yet, if I may again be theological, I would suggest that we are not alone; we are not the only ones minding the store. The universe is immensely thick. We are, compared to the reality out there, like a bug: a praying mantis who is addressing the United Nations! The bug gets up there, he looks out and says: "Huh! Not much food out there!" And that is all he thinks! Nothing about the machinations of nations and the intrigues of the history of civilizations. We are that bug in terms of the reality out there and what we perceive of it! But having, at the same time, a nostalgia for transcendence, and probably having coded in ourselves an extraordinary availability of knowledge.

You have at least thirteen billion brain cells, many more billions internuncial cells, and millions upon millions of internal proprioceptors. We use not five percent or ten percent, but an infinite, fractional decimal of that. Why the hell are we so overendowed? We do not need this stuff! I believe we are so overendowed because we have the capacity to make quantum leaps to new forms and structures of being.

The world is thickening. We are coming to a flowering of global civilization. Let me put it this way: embryos, blastospheres. The blastosphere quickens the next stuff, which then quickens the next stuff. You have little, incidental tribes; they quicken and form small nations and cultures; those quicken to form larger civilizations. These larger civilizations then prime the next stage, like embryos, until you come to the stage we are now reaching: global civilization. After global civilization—what?

Barbara: Universal life.

Jean: But of a form we are priming. It is a larger reality, a larger ecology of things. The larger ecology of things does not make distinctions the way we do: right/wrong, male/female, this/that. Paradox and irony—wherever you want to find the gods, look where the absurd is. Paradox and irony are inherent in these kinds of forms. These forms are quickening, and we are entering into—we are not only entering, we are being entered into as well—a new phase of global consciousness.

Barbara: Yes, I believe that.

Jean: And we are not the only ones minding the store. There is a new paradigm beginning to emerge. We can quicken it—or destroy ourselves in refusing it. But we have primed the next phase just as the blastosphere primes the next phase of the embryo. We are entering into universal life. But I get a little nervous sometimes with the idea of space colonies. Not that I don't think it's a very interesting idea, but the idea is not rich enough. That's the old thinking—the idea that we move from *here* to *there*. Probably we move from *here* to *here*. All the current pop culture that says: We come from the stars!—and the cargo cult mythos of flying saucers—it isn't rich enough. The reality is probably much, much deeper. We probably come from the depths. And the depths are rising to nurture and sustain us. What is happening, we do not know. We can grope with agricultural images, with poetic images, with metaphors . . . I like to use the little joke that a man's reach must exceed his grasp, or what's a meta-phor? *[laughter]*

You know, Barbara, I'm one of those women who, like you, never used to talk to women.

Barbara: Curiously enough, everyone that interests me now is a woman.

Jean: I'm finding, too, that now that's all changed. Why? I think that probably this thickening reality is entering more right now through women than men because *we* don't have the old paradigms.

Hazel: We don't have the old programs!

Jean: We weren't allowed paradigms. Being on the outside really helps! Adversity!

Hazel: That's right! Yesterday I received the nicest gift that I have received from a man in a long time. A friend of mine said to me that Alfred North Whitehead had said that the most interesting and innovative members of the human species were self-educated women. For all of these reasons, of course. We have no intellectual or emotional investment.

Jean: That is why you can perceive the emergent paradigms. It's not even a paradigm; it's a metadigm.

Hazel: Or it's a misty outline of something.

Jean: Well, mysticism—it is misty-schisms, of course.

Barbara: About this rising of the depths—let me explain my attraction to space colonies in this context. It started with what I think of as an "expanded reality" experience. I was taking a walk one day in 1966 and asked myself a question: What in our age is comparable to the birth of Christ? Then I went on autodrive in a semi daydream, walking around the hill, losing track of time and space. Suddenly the blue cocoon of Earth opened up. My mind's eye was on the moon and I literally felt myself as a cell in the body of our planet Earth. I sensed an answer—We are being born into the universe! We have a birth to announce. It is our own. We—our whole planetary body—was struggling to coordinate; pain was coursing through the whole system; we were running out of energy, gasping for breath, reaching into space toward the sun. With that reach outward I felt a profound interlinking of all the other cells on the body of the planet—I call it the "synergizing Earth." We felt ourselves as one body. It was euphoric. And somehow I also sensed the presence of "other life"— benign intelligences that were so near I could almost communicate with them, but not quite, perhaps like a newborn baby senses its mother and father, but its nervous system is still too immature to see. Ever since that experience, I have known intuitively that the human species will become universal. As we develop cosmic consciousness we will also develop the capacity for cosmic action—we are not a one-planet species. Our space program is an infantile description of a natural capacity of a universal species. I believe that cosmic consciousness and action are concurrent, interdependent abilities—just as a baby must reach outward toward the world beyond the womb in order to coordinate internally and mature its awareness.

But recently, something new has begun to happen to me . . . that's why I am so happy to be here with both of you. After the [American] Bicentennial, which was a fervor of activity for me, I began to experience a sort of psychic withdrawal. I became depressed. Something was telling me to Stop! Listen! Be still! So I'm finding myself seriously trying to meditate. I'm not at all yet sufficiently deep to find the new signals, but I am turning to myself, to that higher self, and saying: "Guide me. Lead me." I then use my intellect to figure out the intuitions. But they're not quite clear enough for me to know whether they are will, pride, intellect—or genuine. So I find myself working out feedback systems to check out these things. And because I am so highly motivated, I can't turn off. I seem to have a turned-up engine that is always going. If I stop, I flood, literally. My biceps hurt—I have got to keep going.

Jean: Let's try an experiment, an experiential metaphor. Close your eyes. I want you to try to find the nearest technological image for the way you are in the world. Come up with a metaphor . . .

Hazel: The closest I can come is a chemical image. I see myself as an enzyme, a bridge person, a catalytic exchanger.

Jean: Very good. Now keep your eyes closed and hold that image. Intensify it. Let it begin to yeast through your system and see what it does to your body, to your mind, to your heartbeat. . . . What do you note?

Hazel: Bringing together two loose ends . . . with my fingers.

Barbara: The image I've been having is really not a technological image. It's the image of a fetus wrapped up in a kind of placenta in my head. It looks like the image at the end of the movie *2001*.

Jean: Very good. You have both done the next stage of the exercise, not the first stage. The fact is, both of you run at sixty, like turned-up engines. That's the way you live. And when you are dealing with this kind of stress you have no time for input. What I would ask you to do is to accept as an assumption of faith that you have this enormous instrumentation. It is an ecological instrumentation: not merely the billions of brain cells, but there are also leaky margins. There is a tremendous amount of information coming at you. It would mean to switch—as if you were turning a switch—into another mode of being. In this mode you are not the go-getter; you are not the mother of the universe who is healing everybody. You become a receptor.

Now, if you were to have that image of receptor, and all of a sudden turn the switch, a whole new system of receptivity would be there to feed you that has nothing to do with the engine structure of pride, will, chutzpah, or whatever. You are in a different realm of experience, a realm of receptivity in which all the internal proprioceptors and brain cells that you are not using are plugged into a system that will nurture you for a new time. Different kinds of analogues and images begin to flood you. You have been loaded with an enormous amount of information, but it's operating on certain expectations and variables regardless of how creative a thinker you are.

Our culture gives us that particular mind/bodyscape. Use the metaphor of switching to a level where loves, jealousies, lusts, passions, wills, fears, and vulnerability do not operate. It's like being in a different dimension of being. You no longer have to ask Who? or What? or Where? Your images—the fetus, the image of bridging—are already images of validity for you. We are talking about a level of deep identity—another realm that is always accessible, even if you are in the center of a noisy conference. And you will be fed from that level. You will perceive a great deal of new information—and the emergent paradigms! Very simply, you enter a much larger universe.

Barbara: Jean, may I ask you what you see when you do this exercise?

Jean: I have an image of a hive, a wonderful beehive. It's millions of miles deep, and each part of the hive as I look in is a totally different reality. I am on the inside of it, and am getting the ambiance from the totality of all these different realities. It then leads me to live in two worlds. It's like being in a realm of the gods, and a realm here. You always say, Barbara, that I am very powerful, but it's not really that. It's that I am a transducer for other realms of reality. The sacred is always where there is presence, and as you become a channel for larger realities you become . . . Present. And each moment becomes a spiritual exercise. Each moment becomes loaded, and open, and you interact with many other moments in the most serendipitous and synchronistic way.

Barbara: When you choose your acts, as you are very active in the world— tell me how you choose what to do. Or perhaps the acts choose you. But how do you design your activity in relationship to this other awareness that is flooding you?

Jean: A lot of acts choose one. When you enter into a realm of organism-environment, and you do what you have to do in your regular life—be it remaking a house, or doing an experiment, or giving a talk—then you are in such a state of resonance that the essential realities that are emerging begin to choose you. You don't know who is the chooser, and who the chosen. Are you the dancer?—or are you being danced? And it doesn't make any difference. You don't lose your will; your will just becomes much, much larger. You're not just existentially willful.

Hazel: That really is a lovely image, isn't it?

II

"We Mustn't Try to Find Our Paradigms in Conventional Forms, Be They Eastern or Western"

*Right Livelihood, Right Politics. The court-jester role.
Beyond ego and identity needs. Recomposting human values
and contributing to evolutionary potential. The evolutionary
way: breaking into the infinite. "New worlds on Earth, new worlds in
space." Internal empowerment and modes of interior existence.*

Jean: I would like to ask Hazel a question that I think will lead us back to our discussion of female consciousness. What changes have you experienced in your pattern of thinking, sense of the possible, sense of yourself in the world? What are the changes that have occurred in the last five or ten years? Is there a difference?

Hazel: Oh yes, a tremendous difference. First of all, I'm no longer operating out of insecurity. I had a tremendous desire during the first half of the past ten years to prove myself because of not having gone to college. I wanted to express myself, and I wanted to be listened to. I knew that the hurdle I had to overcome was this thing about being an uneducated housewife. My ego at that time was at a stage where it could be absolutely demolished—to the point of pulling the covers over my head and doing absolutely nothing. That began to be solved for me maybe about three years ago when I started getting enough feedback from what I was writing to feel the courage to be sure of myself.

I have now come to a stage where I really don't care. I know that I have to unfold. I know that I am the bearer of a small piece of evolutionary potential and that it has to be expressed. What I'm trying to do now is to get beyond the ego need aspect of it. Someone who has been very helpful to me since I've known him is Fritz Schumacher, the man who wrote *Small Is Beautiful*.[1] His mode of operating out of humility has been very inspiring. If you can make yourself very small and quiet, and do it anyway, you find that it is a tremendously sustainable way to be. You don't flare up like a roman candle and burn out. I have been very active in citizen-organizing types of things, and I've seen so many of my young friends over the past ten years just burn out. It was all to do with pride, ego, and identity needs.

At one point I began to read a lot of books about the crusading personality! And so although I basically like crusading, and know that I'm good at it, I knew that I would have to relax and realize that there should be no goal to crusading. What I'm trying to do is to give up goals. Goals are very hubristic. I know that if I am chasing goals my daughter will have to spend a lot of her life undoing the goal that I've achieved.

What I'm trying to do now is to phase myself more and more with the energies around me. The role that I'm going to try to play is not only the role of Right Livelihood, which I find very satisfying, but also the role that I call Right Politics. Right Politics is the next stage from Right Livelihood. I do have an instrumental will; I'm not going to throw it away or deny it.

I'm going to take full responsibility for it. For me, Right Politics is being a court jester. You try to gain access to situations where the powerful have been making decisions behind closed doors, and try to raise their levels of awareness about what they're doing. I'm learning all the psychological tricks to reveal to them their own instrumental rationality, their own ego needs; to make them aware of how much is due to identity and how much is due to the real search for the truth.

One of the things that I find is very useful to do in scientific groups, for example, is to suggest that maybe we shouldn't give Nobel Prizes anymore for some of the dangerous areas like DNA research and nuclear physics. Then we would at least make sure that the aims of those people working in these fields would stem from the selfless search for the truth and not ego and identity needs. Instead we could give Nobel Prizes to people who are developing philosophies of science.

I see my role here as helping this recomposting of human culture that is going on now, and contributing of human culture that is going on now, and contributing to evolutionary potential in this mode while trying not to get hung up in the whole idea of timescales and schedules. The idea that, my God—the revolution had be accomplished by—

Barbara: 1976!

[laughter]

Hazel: If only you begin to see time as a hubristic thing. The human being is the measuring rod. It doesn't matter when it happens. The point is that maybe I'll be around for another twenty or thirty years, if I'm lucky, and I'll do this thing because that's the way I'm set up to do it. It doesn't matter what's accomplished in my lifetime, or in my daughter's lifetime, or whether the millennium or the noosphere will be achieved a thousand million years from now. I love the idea that human beings may have cycled many times before; and that we have reached this technological fifth stage and may have blown it: and that maybe this is the twelfth time around, or maybe the twentieth. It just makes you cool out. I can only function by getting rid of the anxiety I used to have. I'm realizing that human evolution is a long march and we are not to know where it leads.

Jean: How would you answer the same question, Barbara? What has happened to you in terms of a deepening change in sensibility?

Barbara: I have been slow in my development, and yet it's always been the same in a curious way. I started out with, and still have, a deep-seated attraction to something that's coming. I lived with a deep sense of expectancy that I had no way of living out in my role of mother. Eventually I began to find the evolutionary way, and I became joyful. I sensed the linkage between my life and the entire past. I began to feel a speeding up of the evolutionary process, and it literally turned up that engine in me. I could feel kinesthetically something going faster. I related strongly to the birth image. There is a timing in organic events even though we might not be able to judge that timing.

I was sure that something new was coming, and that it had to do with the universe, and with transcendence.

When the space program came along I felt a great surge of excitement because I saw the reality of breaking into the infinite in real terms, both physically and spiritually. It affirmed the birth experience. When the lunar landing occurred in 1969 the world seemed to have a shared experience—it was almost like the "synergizing Earth." For one brief moment, were united in a transcendent awareness that our species has a common destiny in the universe. There was a joyful feeling throughout our "body" that something had happened. But then, despair deepened. It was the time of Vietnam, urban riots, drug abuse. The media communicated pain. The environmentalists communicated limits—only limits. There didn't seem to be any voices of hope. I really feared that we might destroy ourselves for lack of awareness of the direction of hope. The fact was that if we could coordinate our total capacities harmoniously, we were on the brink of the greatest age in human history—foreseen by the saints and seers of our species.

Also, through the birth experiences I sensed that we were at a time when rapid, concurrent coordination of many functional elements was vital for survival: We had to stop polluting our environment, move quickly toward a better distribution of material goods throughout our body politic, identify new functions for people who felt useless, young and old, develop new sources of energy before the fossil fuels ran out. It felt sort of like a viability test—a judgment of this phase of life. If we were seriously defective in any major system, the whole body might die.

I felt another deep commandment: "Put this purpose first, before your husband, your children, yourself." I had to find a way to communicate the good news that we're being born, not dying.

At that time we formed the Committee for the Future to identify and communicate the positive opportunities for the future, not just in the space program, but in all fields.

Then in 1974 I began to feel a powerful desire to enter the political arena—on a "platform of the whole"—involving people in stating their goals, interacting with each other and with futurists, and coming up with viable solutions to our collective problems. I wanted to run for the presidency on a new kind of campaign based on a feeling that Teilhard de Chardin describes in *Building the Earth*—the sense that every man, woman and child is need to build "new worlds in space." But I quickly realized it was impossible. To organize such an effort I would have to become an adversary, join one political party, raise millions of dollars . . . And besides, I wasn't prepared.

During the Bicentennial, we organized a large international SYNCON— a conference in the round—with people calling in from all over the country with their goals. Everyone got very excited. I felt it was the next step of democracy in utero. But again, it was premature. I was suddenly exhausted, depressed. I had been so excited by the idea of people from all over the world connecting together to manifest the joy of integration; I had literally felt in my body the joy of people coming together. It excited me so, and I loved it so, that I had gotten overly turned on by the idea of trying to manifest it in physical terms.

Jean: The last time the Word became flesh it ended up on the cross!
[laughter]

Barbara: What we did was nice, but it had nothing to do with the vision I had. I realized it was premature, and too external. And of course, we had failed financially. It was such an interesting exertion that I lost my motivation. I couldn't think of anything that I wanted to do. My compass of joy turned off. I scanned the horizon . . . and there was no magnetism.

Hazel: But that was so good for you, Barbara.

Barbara: Well, I began to inner signals telling me to relax, take it easy, very much kind of thing you've been talking about, Jean. Something from within was saying, "We are with you; there is a library of consciousness and you can tune in to anything you want; it's happening if you will just relax, if you will just *be*." I was so close—I am so close—to that happening. Then I began to think that if I'm supposed to just be, then thank God I don't have to do anything! I was really delighted not to do anything. I would have been happy to die, to sit; or I would have been happy to whatever I was told.

So what I really wanted to do at that point was to cut loose and roam the planet; to visit, and talk, and feel. But I had received this money, and I had inherited from my past activities in the television-audio field people and facilities. I had, and continue to have, a deep sense of the voices of creativity all over the planet needing to be connected; to be heard, not only by each other, but by the larger number of human beings who are incipiently evolving but need a trigger. And the trigger is a voice.

I began to feel that I should invest this money in the establishment of a radio network that would pick up the voices of creativity and evolution and send them out into the mainstream continually. So I tried to meditate on this feeling to find out if the feeling was correct. I sensed that a fundamental sickness on our planet is our mass media; it's an infantile nervous system picking up and communicating only the pain—the breakdown rather than the breakthrough. We could fail for lack of awareness of our potentials.

I had been so mistaken about timing before, and suddenly here I was again, about to charge into a major act based on an inner feeling, but requiring organization, power—the power to implement, not power over people. And I found many people wanting to do this with me.

Right now I am in a very strange state, the strangest state I've ever been in. This radio network is almost set up, but it's all men who want to do it. There are women as well, of course, but it's all men who happen to have the necessary technical skills. We may even have quite a few outlets that would make it economically viable over and above the investment I can put into it. Inside, however, I am almost paralyzed. I have been given the external empowerment to do this thing, but really through no volition of my own.

Jean: And you don't get the internal empowerment.

Barbara: No. But an abundance of external empowerment. And an abundance of internal motivation. But not empowerment. And so here I am, with all these people, and all this money . . .

Jean: It's ironic, isn't it? For many years all of the patterns that you have been investing in and structuring have all come home to roost with this radio thing. I was always about voices, connections, networking. And finally the consummation, devoutly to be wished at one time, arrives at a time when you no longer wish it. Whereas the internal patterns, which you did not pursue because of so much objectification of the world, have now risen up and said, "It is our turn." We create our realities all the time, you know. The ironic situation—and it can be tragic, but we must see that it merely becomes tragicomic, which means a happy ending—is that you end up with the external empowerment, but without the internal wherewithal to do anything about it.

Barbara: That's it.

Jean: It seems evident that you have got to put in an intense space-time period—it might just be a month—in which the depth levels can yeast.

Barbara: I know that, Jean. And I say in all vulnerability that I need help. I would be willing to stop the Futures Network tomorrow if it's not what I'm supposed to do. Actually I don't like most of the things I have to do because they're organizational things. I have the feeling that if I were able to reach deeper levels of myself the network would actually be very easy. But when I sit down to mediate I'm too self-conscious.

Jean: Well, it's also because your pattern of life is to be given unto. It's a dialogical pattern with others. This is one of the problems with being female: one tends to think in dialogues. Not everyone, of course, but this happens very frequently. It is dialogue that has provided you with the spiritual juices, or the psychological juices. All of a sudden there's this lonely, solipsistic universe where you're all by yourself.

Barbara: Yes, and no one can tell me what to do.

Jean: Unless you people the depths.

Barbara: People the depths?

Jean: With archetypes. With Wise Old Ladies! Or Wise Old Man!—in a good Jungian kind of structure.

Barbara: I'm ready to do that, if I could find them. And I am listening. Ben Bentof sent me a little book called *The Impersonal Life* in which there is phrase: "Be still and know I am God." This is a book written by Your Higher Self. If you are still, the Higher Self will take over. I'm trying to be still and let that happen.

Jean: But maybe your mode of stillness is noisy.

Barbara: I think it is.

Jean: Maybe you should be saying, "Hey, H. S.! Yoo-hoo!" *[laughter]* No,

I really mean that!—to invoke. You've always been invocatory. There is a Buddhist way of being quiet, but you don't look very Buddhist to me.

Barbara: I'm not Buddhist! I'm a Jewish mother!

Jean: And the Jewish mother has never been known to be still! *[laughter]*

Barbara: Do you think I could call out loud, "Higher Self: Walk with me! Talk with me!"?

Jean: Yes! I think it's invocative. You're dramatic; you're theatrical. And the modes of interior existence vary enormously. That's why we must not try to find our paradigms in kosher forms, be they Eastern or Western.

III

"The Gift Is Given"

*The experimental mode of knowing. Accelerating
creative processes. Core experiences: the vital interrelatedness
of all things and the capacity to know everything. We are "gods-
in-making." Images of the future: ecological and psychological
science fiction. Rebalancing inner and outer space. Unus Mundus.*

*After the preceding conversation, we moved
into the dining room for lunch—sans tape recorders.
Scarcely had we been seated, however, before I was
rushing off to find a portable model so as
not to miss the following. As the tape resumes,
Jean is talking about the nature of reality. Imagine,
if you will, background sound effects attendant
to the breaking of bread . . .*

Jean: If you take a group of, say, one hundred passages from famous mystics about the nature of reality, and you compare them with an equal number of passages by modern physicists in the Einstein–Heisenberg mode, you can't tell them apart!

Hazel: This is what Fritjof Capra talks about in that marvelous book *The Tao of Physics*.[2]

Jean: Yes! You cannot tell a quantum perspective on the nature of space-time from St. Teresa's notions of spiritual dimensions. Isn't there a level of consciousness at which metaphors just give up, and you're faced with the reality itself?

Hazel: Yes, and the whole differentiation thing becomes the problem.

Barbara: I'm wondering, Jean, if part of the new beingness is going to transcend existing scientific method to become an experiential way of knowing—which doesn't discard logic, and doesn't discard what we can verify externally, but amplifies it through a superintuitive form of knowing. This would be what Erich Jantsch called *syntony*—picking up the evolutionary process as a higher form of intuitive knowing. Not exactly mystical visions; but, for example, actually becoming atoms in order to find out how atoms work—you are atoms, after all. I would call this evolutionary consciousness—a synthesis of mystical and secular consciousness. Now that we are becoming responsible for our planetary evolution, we must become more aware of the evolutionary process; it's too complex to "know" from a purely intellectual perspective.

Hazel: Yes, actually experiencing it in a direct way. . . . Barbara, will you help yourself to some cheese?

Barbara: Thank you, I will. I'm talking about experiencing atoms, molecules, cells; experiencing the biosphere. It's like knowing our own bodies—hunger, pain, sleepiness, sexual attraction . . . If we had to read books to know all those things, we would simply die. I was talking recently to Ted Taylor, who is a very conscientious scientist, and he told me that there was no way that he could make a certain judgment about books about the use of nuclear energy. The complexities were so elaborate that there was simply no way of getting all the knowledge needed to make the judgment. So he said: "I have to go by the seat of my pants!"

Jean: That's called, technically, *glutei maximi,* kinesthetic knowing! *[laughter]*

I did an experiment with six very famous scientists, one of whom was a Nobel Prize winner. They had come to me and said, "Look, we're all in frontier areas of science"—aging, molecular biology, and so on—"and we would like to know, since you've done all this work on the psychology and phenomenology of creativity, if you could induce in us various creative states common to highly creative people."This would mean such things as imagistic thinking, played out almost like plays, of whatever is the object of their pursuit. Different states of consciousness—enormous, elated, enthusiastic states. Deep trance states. States that typically happen when there are highly creative procedures going on. Would this begin to accelerate the creative process? I said that I didn't know, but that it might.

Barbara: They had come to you?

Jean: Yes. And so we decided to try, and began to work with these people. They were horrible subjects for the most part. They would fall asleep because it would reverse their analytic mode. But about four out of the six became very good. And sure enough, they found themselves working in these altered states of consciousness. For example, one of them, who was working on aging, had been working on the thymus gland. He found himself in a very intricate morality play—a mystery play—in the enzymes. He was one of the enzymes, and the other enzymes were other parts. The most extraordinary dance and moral drama began to unfold. He began to realize that the story that was unfolding in this level of imagery was actually the story of a remarkable synthesis of enzymes and interactions that had to do with the aging process. He came out of this and said: "My God, I would need a whole new biological calculus to be able to deal with this!" And he ran back to Rockefeller University and started to work on it.

Four out of the six now believe that by getting into internal structures, and using this ready instrumentation—imagery at high affect states of consciousness—the creative process can in fact be accelerated. With so much of our science it is a question of state-dependent learning! A scientist does his work in a certain analytic, rational state; and yet most of the great breakthroughs occur by virtue of a suspension of that particular mindscape. So in giving them the same kind of internal ways of working that you find in people with sustained creativity, we found that it did indeed accelerate the creative process. Instead of taking five years, it took several months. This is of course something that people have always known, but have for the most part ignored.

Barbara: Do you think, Jean, that as a species we might be evolving naturally towards that form of knowing? Now it has to be more or less induced.

Jean: Any child can do it.

Barbara: Yes, but it is educated out of them.

Jean: No, it can never be educated out.

Hazel: But it can be blocked.

Jean: Greatly blocked. So much of my education was a systematic forgetting of everything I knew that was really important. Especially in the Catholic schools.

Hazel: And how did you get into the process of recapturing it?

Jean: Well, I went to twenty-nine schools before I was twelve. Daddy was writing *The Bob Hope Show,* and Bob was always on the road, so we were always moving. I was educated in the classical tradition by my mother on the train, which meant that you learned whole plays of Shakespeare, reams of poetry, and Italian operas. History was something that went by at eighty miles an hour.

Barbara: So in some deep sense you're self-educated.

Jean: Yes. But I'm glad I didn't get stuck in St. Ephraim's School in Brooklyn!

Hazel: Of course, you have to have a very strong sense of yourself to resist that. Both of my parents were atheists, which, for me, was very fortunate. I can remember, for instance, coming home from school one day when I was about six, and telling my mother that we had learned about the little Lord Jesus that day. And she said: "Rubbish!" *[laughter]* And so when you grow up in that sort of atmosphere, you know that you'd better put it all together for yourself!

Barbara: Well, I had that same sort of experience. When I asked my father what he thought about God, he said: "I don't know; you find out." He was a pure agnostic, and has always been very open, which was helpful. Was your father religious, Jean?

Jean: Well, you asked me how I got where I am, and it's all to do with that. My father was an agnostic Baptist, and that he remained until he was eighteen years old and fell in love with Bethy Lou Schultz, who was an Episcopalian. So he became an Episcopalian. And then he fell in love with Maudy Bullet, who was a Presbyterian. So he became a Presbyterian. He came to New York, fell in love with my mother—who was a first-generation Sicilian Catholic, born in Siracusa—and those people you marry! *[laughter]*

So he had to go to religious instruction school. He was a comedy writer, of course, so he and the young priest at St. Patrick's used to trade jokes. And finally the priest said: "Ah, Jack, you're just a natural-born pagan! Here, I'll give you a learner's permit so you can get married. But you've got to bring the kid up Catholic." "Sure, sure," says my father, and he was married.

Now, when I came along, my father was in one of his broke periods, so we found ourselves for one year in what my grandmother referred to as "Brook-a-leena"—the Sicilian section of Brooklyn! And I was sent to St. Ephraim's Catholic School. The problem was, my daddy would try to gag up my catechism. He would give me the most interesting questions to ask the poor nun in the morning. Like, "Sister Theresa, Sister Theresa, I counted Joey Manginello's ribs, and I counted my ribs, and we have the same number of ribs. Now what I want to know is, if God made Eve from Adam's rib . . ." *[laughter]* Or, the one that torments the mind of every small child: "Sister Theresa, did Jesus ever have to go to the bathroom?" *[laughter]*

Well, Sister Theresa finally blew up. She had, as I remember, this very curious lisp. And she said: "Blaschphemy! Blaschphemy! Scharilledge and blaschphemy!" *[laughter]* And she went and got out oak tag, got out India ink, got out tacks, got out a chair, jumped up on the chair, tacked up the oak tag and wrote, "Jean Houston's Years in Purgatory!" And every time I asked the wrong question: a big X. X represented a hundred thousand years in Purgatory! *[laughter]* At the end of the first grade, when I turned six, I had three hundred million years in Purgatory to my credit! *[laughter]*

Well, on the day of the great addition I went home crying and sobbing and believing all this stuff. And my father says: "What's the matter, kiddo? You ran into the trolley car and the cookies in your pocket got mashed!" No! "You're turning green, your feet are taking root, and you think you've caught the chestnut blight!" No! Finally I said, "Daddy, you don't understand! I've got to go to Purgatory for three hundred million years and it's all your fault!" My father screamed with laughter and said, "Great, Honeypot! Keep that up and we'll put you on the air next to Henny Youngman!" And then he picked me up, and started to make the sound of an engine chugging along the track: "Purgatory-purgatory-purgatory-purgatory, toot-toot! Purgatory-purgatory-purgatory . . . Here comes the Purgatory Special!" *[laughter]*

And he leaps downstairs, flying past the Sicilian neighbors, who say, "Ah, dere gosa crazy Jack!" And he says to me: "You think you've got problems, kiddo? Wait till you see how they hog-tied poor old Bernadette." So he took me to a movie that was playing at the time, called *The Song of Bernadette*, starring Jennifer Jones. And the theater was packed with Sicilian Catholics. A nice little old lady in black was seated next to us and every time Jennifer Jones would appear on the screen, she would cross herself, saying, "*Ah, che bella questa Santa.*" What a beautiful saint. Then comes the great moment. The Virgin Mary, a vision of luminous white, appears in the grotto; and we're all in a rapture of true devotion. All the little old ladies were saying: "*Santa Vergine! Santa Vergine!*" All of a sudden this horrible, whinnying, mulelike laughter began to fill the theater—just at the holy moment! And it was coming from my father! I was horrified. "Daddy," I said, "quiet! This is the holy part!" "I know, Honeypot," he said. "But do you know who that is up there on the screen? That's old Linda Darnell! We met her last year at that party in Beverly Hills. Hot dog, I told her she'd go far!" And he let out this wild laughter that he couldn't control.

The little old ladies were all saying: "*Diavolo! Diavolo!*" "Daddy please!" I said. "Go to the bathroom!" So he got up and came back a little later. He was pretty good—a few snorts to remind us of his true feelings. But on the way home I didn't want anything to do with him; I wouldn't even let him take my hand to cross the street. "Daddy, just go away!" I said. "I'm going to see the Virgin." "Oh. Okay," he said. "I'll go with you." And then—I will never forget this—he tried to pull me into this horrible Dorothy and the Tin Man routine. He started to sing: "We're off to see the Virgin, the wonderful Virgin of Lords. . . . We'll join the hordes and hordes and hordes—" "Daddy, will you go away!"

And I ran home, and straight up to the second floor, where there was this huge closet with a wall safe in the back. It was empty because Chickie the dog had had her eight puppies there. So I pulled out the dog, put out the pups, fell to my knees, and eyed the wall safe. "Virgin Mary," I said. "Uh, will you please appear to me like you did to Bernadette? I'll give up . . . cookies for a week!" *[laughter]* "Two weeks, okay? I'll count to ten and you be there." I counted to ten, opened my eyes, but no Virgin Mary. "Um, Virgin Mary? This time I'll count to twenty-seven, and you be there. Okay?" So I counted to twenty-seven, opened my eyes, but no Virgin Mary. This went on and on, until I finally said, "Virgin Mary? Maybe you don't know where I live. It's number 14-4 Avenue O and Eddie Canzaneri is jumping rope downstairs. Now, I'll count to a hundred sixty-seven and you be there. Okay?"

I closed my eyes and began to count, feeling quite sure that she would make it this time. I had a vision in my head of the Virgin Mary like some great white bird flapping over the Brooklyn Bridge, looking for my house. One hundred and sixty-seven! My eyes flew open. No Virgin Mary. Chickie had all the pups back in the closet, nursing happily. So I got up and went over to the window and looked out at the fig tree in the yard. And I gave up. Totally gave up! I must have done something right, though, because then it happened. Nothing happened externally, but in that moment of totally giving up, the whole universe moved into meaning. I knew absolutely that I, and the fig tree in the yard, the pups in the closet, and my ideal of the Virgin Mary were all part of an extraordinary, orchestral . . . *music* would be the only analogue. It was like a symphony. Everything was vitally related to everything else, and it was all moving together. And it was very, very good. Now, downstairs at that moment, my father came into the house. And he was laughing. And the whole universe began to laugh. The fig tree laughed, a rainbow tittered . . .

All I can think of is that great image at the end of Dante's *Paradiso*: the joy that spins the universe! It was like an extraordinarily powerful, orchestral coding. And so powerful was that experience that it has remained central to my whole life. I knew in that moment that we were capable of knowing everything; we were capable of being in the interstices of things, of being both reflector and reflected.

Barbara: And so you went on to discover intellectually what you had experienced as a child.

Jean: Yes, I did. I now know that we have the actual instrumentation for these other forms of knowing. But my father was a critical part of this, because every time I tried to confront a dogma, he broke it up with laughter. It was like a constant series of comical Zen koans. Everything was broken up. We all talk about core experiences, well that certainly was mine.

Barbara: Did you ever have any kind of core experience, Hazel, that has guided your life as the "birth experience" has guided mine?

Hazel: No. But I have always felt—and this probably sounds almost prideful— that I was capable of knowing everything.

Jean: And why not?

Hazel: Well, you know, the whole educational thing tells you that you're ignorant. But I've always felt that I was part of the whole, and that it was only a matter of what I chose to pay attention to. How you expressed yourself was one thing, but you were always connected back to the largest totality of everything that I could imagine.

I've never really developed religious metaphors. The only one I've ever had was the one I learned from my mother: the pantheistic metaphor. She would show me where she would like to be buried when she dies—her favorite rose bed. She had all of those lovely sorts of images: that we were all part of the same thing anyway, and that when you died part of you would be in a cloud, and part of you in a flower. That's really the only imagery I've ever related to. And also the time dimension of that. I've always felt that my molecules were in Julius Caesar, and so on. The whole thing is just one ball of wax.

In some ways I felt that that was almost anti-intellectual. It was very difficult to learn to operate in the logical-positivist mode. But if you're coming off of a nondifferentiated kind of awareness, then all of the disciplines, and all of the submicroscopic information and mapping in those disciplines becomes so easy and simple because you can see it as a tiny little module of knowledge.

And the other thing is that you know how far you need to delve into a discipline in order to communicate with those folks who were socialized in that way. You don't need to go to all of the depths of baroque elaboration of the subsystems in order to have dialogue with them. It's like learning a certain amount of French in order to be able to talk to French people. You learn enough to be able to communicate with them and to know what's wrong with the paradigm and where it fits into a much larger scheme of things.

What I find disturbing is that the way I know the planet, the universe, and my place in it, is quite beyond language.

Barbara: Sounds like she's in the hive too. This is a very abstract metaphysical question, but somehow it matters a lot to me. Do you feel that the universe is evolving towards something that it—the whole—has not yet been? Or do you see it as something fully created, and sort of turning around and playing with itself?

Hazel: I see it pulsating and I love Everett's "many worlds" interpretation. The way I play off this is with the idea of keywording our way through the great universal computer program—creating our own thing as we go along. I can't buy the big bang theory; I see everything in cycles. The whole thing is pulsating.

Barbara: Never sort of escalating in its pulses?

Hazel: No. It's a timeless—

Jean: But in its pulsation it may become something else. It's never the same thing. We were not sitting here ten billion aeons ago.

Hazel: Oh no, it's never the same thing. It's always different patterns, like a kaleidoscope.

Barbara: I sense, too, that it's pulsating, but I also sense a progressiveness in its pulsation.

Jean: An enrichment.

Barbara: Yes, an enriching, an enhancing, an increasing of consciousness.

Jean: Also, you see, individuals in it can then be spun off from it.

Barbara: I'm not talking about any ordinary form of progress here.

Jean: You're talking about process.

Barbara: Process that enriches as it progresses to higher levels of synthesis and organization.

Jean: This might be similar to the bodhisattva view, which is that you don't go off into nirvana until the last little blade of grass is evolved. Perhaps it's this same kind of thing, and we are all in this process of enrichment. We then gain much more responsibility for creation and creativity ourselves. We are not just gods-in-hiding; we are gods-in-making.

Hazel: And we give it back to another part of the system.

Jean: We give it back, and we become responsible. This relates to the problem of death. I myself no longer believe in death, or in birth. They're all transitions.

Hazel: Yes, exactly.

Jean: I don't think that this is a sunlit journey to a sunless shore. Some form of my persona continues and grows, and I've been emerging—I have distant memories, both backward and forward.

Barbara: Tell me about the memories forward.

Jean: The memories back, I must say, are much clearer because I've accepted that. *[laughter]* When I was three years old I remember walking around kicking the Ford cars. Kicking them! And my father would say, "Why are doin' that? That's good rubber!" And I would answer, "Because where I come from we did it so much better. We didn't need this!"

Hazel: That's amazing.

Barbara: You were three?

Jean: But many two- and three-year-olds come up with this kind of notion. It's as if it were a memory forward.

Barbara: I know exactly what you mean. I feel as if I'm living in the past right now.

Jean: In archaic forms! Whether true or not, most of us feel we are slugging it out in a very archaic—not even archaic, that's too good a word for it—anachronistic culture.

Hazel: A rearview mirror culture.

Jean: All the horrors of H. G. Wells' time machine—guess what! We're caught in one! *[laughter]*

Hazel: Yes, we're caught in one!

Barbara: We definitely share this perception of reality—of being in an anachronistic culture, in something we know is inferior because we must have experienced something forward.

Jean: Or, forget about back and forward. It might be to the side. Our notions of space and time are very linear. The structure of grammar affects the structure of experience; thus when you say space-time we all get nauseous because it goes against our grammar.

Barbara: I would like to ask you, Jean, whether you have specific images of the future. Don't use the word *future* if it is too linear.

Jean: I don't even have to talk about my own images; I can talk about what is emerging. We don't allow prophesy in our culture, so it goes underground and comes up as science fiction. In the 1880s and '90s, the mode of science fiction was hardware science fiction: the ship to the moon, the ship under the sea, the laser. In the 1920s and '30s, this becomes manifest. In the '30s and '40s, the cutting edge of science fiction is sociological science fiction: *Brave New World, 1984.* And we're well on our way to that. In the 1960s and '70s, two dominant forms have been emerging: psychological science fiction and ecological science fiction. Consider Robert Heinlein's *Stranger in a Strange Land*, or the books of Carlos Castaneda, or *2001.* Wonderful science fiction! And they're all about mutations or new ways of being. Look at the characters of Castaneda—Don Juan—and Heinlein—Michael Valentine Smith from *Stranger in a Strange Land.* You find that they make use of different sense perceptions—synesthesias. They hear color; they see sound; they touch taste; they taste God; they smell time. They can look in the aroma of a desert flower and perceive galaxies billions of light years away. They have enormous freedom in time and space. They can experience five minutes as ten hours and thus review material that would normally take ten hours in five minutes. Their relationship to machines . . . all of these mythogems take place in modern times, but their relationship to machines is very different. When Don Juan or Michael Valentine Smith are around, machines go haywire, break up, disappear. It's as if they're making use of a different symbiotic ecology to get things done.

I know, from the point of view of what I know about the instrumentation and the fraction that we're using, that a lot of these so-called third-world modes of doing things—be it medicine, be it transportation, be it modes of communication—are resonant in us. But we are so tuned to ourselves as prosthetic extensions that we have lost this enormous amount of knowledge. Anything that you read in Castaneda or in Heinlein we can demonstrate for you in the laboratory. Including having Ford cars appearing and disappearing in the living room, as occurs in Castaneda. That's a very simple thing to do.

Time: we could give you five minutes of clock time to experience hours and hours in which to rehearse your piano, or golf. Because of the very minute synaptical connections that would have been made in a trance state, with intensive imagery of rehearsal, and subjective time distortion, you would come out at the end of five minutes as if you had had ten hours of practice, and you would be that much better. This is something that musicians have always known. We can do this in the laboratory. The brain can process millions of images in microseconds: images have a different time. It's like falling from a cliff, expecting to die, and in that very brief time reexperiencing your entire life—in its own time.

And another thing is that the remembering of the future may already be coded into the potential of ourselves.

Barbara: Let me ask you a question, Jean. If the psychic abilities of travel and communication are inherent and were manifest in earlier cultures—

Jean: And in present cultures.

Barbara: Yes, and were superceded by the scientific technological extensions—

Jean: Not superceded, overwhelmed. Made more dominant.

Barbara: Okay, overwhelmed. Would you say, Jean, that the scientific technological extensions will gradually become nonuseful again?

Jean: Oh no. They'll simply join the great panoply of possibilities. They're not going to be outmoded. But—and you write about this so well, Hazel—the resources are going to run out in fifty years! Why do you suppose people like ourselves are trying to find these alternate modes of being, and to tap the enormous ecology of inner space? The ecological holocaust is twofold: it has to do with the gross overuse of our external environment, and the incredible underuse of internal environment.

Barbara: I think we're faced with two enormous abundances—one being inner, the other outer. The inner is the one you've been talking about: our nervous systems, our bodies, our inner selves.

Jean: The inner may be the same as the outer.

Barbara: Yes, I believe so. I just returned from the AIAA [American Institute of Aeronautics and Astronomics] meeting in Washington, where they were talking about energy from space—solar and so on—and it appears that the resources that will be available to us from outer space are overwhelming if we should decide to make use of them. They are as infinite as the inner. We are not in a resource-short universe: outer space offers an immeasurable resource base for the future. In this sense, there really are no limits to growth. At one and the same moment, while we're recognizing the need for radical change and coordination in the way we've been using both inner and outer resources, we're beginning to sense the infinite on both sides—in both inner and outer space.

Hazel: But as long as we remain hung up on the idea that the resources are only things that we pile up out there, by manipulating the external environment, and not tapping our own resourcefulness, then we're on the wrong track.

Barbara: It's both/and. If you say that we'll tap the inner resources, and have no need for the external possibilities, then you're still missing a vital dimension. It has to be both/and at every step.

Hazel: Yes, it must be both/and. The end of our technological trajectory at the moment is simply the exhaustion of the idea that it's all "out there." It must be a rebalancing of that with the inner resources. If we could build resourcefulness at the rate that Jean is attempting to do it, then there will be a psychic explosion of energy on the planet equal to two hundred thousand nuclear power plants!

All we are really doing, I think, is coming back to the understanding of the universal oneness. If you project the idea of external resources and internal resources to its logical conclusion, all you're really talking about is realigning yourself with the great chi.

Barbara: With the infinite.

Hazel: With everything.

Jean: We are talking about *Unus Mundus*—which we have never experienced. We have never had "inside" ontologically as real as "outside." Until we achieve that, we will have a dying planet.

Great nature is as wide within as without, and the patterns from without can regenerate the patterns from within. And maybe, Barbara, this funny thing that's happening to you with this radio project is trying to generate your within to do something so that it can then say: Yes!

Barbara: Oh, I pray to God that's so! *[laughter]*

Jean: Don't pray! Accept! My child has been given unto you! *[laughter]* But the gift is given, that's another thing we have to say. The gift is given! I was just wondering: How am I different from you ladies? And I realized that you, Hazel, were saying this morning: "We're slugging on! It will eventually come." You've been saying, Barbara: "It's coming! It's coming!" And my view is: It's come!

Barbara: You're in the middle of it.

Jean: I'm in the middle of it; it's in the middle of me; and we dance around.

IV

"The New Form of Eros"

*On becoming cocreators with the creative process.
The world-mind-body continuum: linking the organic
human species body. Making the instrumental
rationality responsible. Monitoring for ego needs and
motivation. "You are the accomplishment." Female
achievements: nonquantifiable, resonance achievements.*

Barbara: Let me pursue this idea we were talking about at lunch—our relationship to the *Unus Mundus*. Our relationship to this, it seems to me, is deepening as we mature. Now, that may mean through many lifetimes, or perhaps through an extended life, which may be an option in the future. This has to do with the symbol of the Tree of Life as being intrinsic to human motivation—of getting to the point where we are in phase with the creative process. If I could define E that expectancy . . .

Someone once asked me, What is the "hunger of Eve"? And I said: Union with God. Not meaning the little god Jehovah—but *union*, deep beingness. The primary drive of human nature has been to know—not only the knowledge of good and evil, but to know the Tree of Life—the invisible processes of creation—how creation works, so we can cooperate with the process. But, as the Genesis story describes it, God prevented the human species from reaching the Tree of Life. He said, if they get there, they'll be like us—immortals, gods. And He expelled the human species from the Garden. But nothing could make us—*Homo sapiens*—the knowing species, stop knowing. We cannot know less; we must know more. So we are approaching the Tree of Life again, and gaining access to the powers of creation and destruction—the atom, the gene, our own brain. It's a cosmic drama. The outcome, I think, depends on whether we in this living generation can learn to love each other as one, and to love "God"—or the creative processes—above all else. With that love we will be able to reach the Tree, to form a deeper union with Creation—to become cocreators.

Jean: Lover and beloved is what you're talking about—the moment of recognition. But if that moment of recognition is not had by you, then it can be dancing all around you, and dancing through you, but you won't see it because you don't experience that level.

Barbara: That's quite possible, but it's also very obvious to me that most people don't see it either, or we wouldn't have a world operating the way it is. I mean, nine out of ten—actually it's much more than that—have never experienced anything even near to that level of union we're talking about or they could not behave in such a manipulative, destructive, ego-centered way. We are talking about the world itself becoming what it could be—what it already is, but has not manifested. We are a warring, destructive people in limited consciousness boxes. How are we going to get out of those boxes? Even if some have in fact gotten beyond that level, most people are still locked in boxes. How do we get out?

The point is that we are a part of the universe, and that our link to it is potential always. Some beings have made the link on a personal level; however, most beings are not making the link. They are still locked in the self-concentration camp. If we truly love and care for the world, there is a natural desire to evoke that linkage. I see this in a lot of your work, Jean: taking the blocks out of people so that they can make the link. And the world itself then becomes something that is much more than if it only happens to you as an individual. If the species does it—and I don't mean every last member of the human species—but if enough members can make the link, then something happens that is much greater than Jean Houston making the link.

Jean: Oh yes, very much so.

Barbara: I would have to express my own motivation as not just Barbara Hubbard making the link, but—well, if that were it I think I would have gone to a mountaintop long ago. I would not be where I am. I believe very deeply that the species as a whole must make the link.

Jean: This is what both of you and myself are all doing—we are evoking linkages in other people. We may be the last to have it in ourselves, but are all very successful in helping to create a world-mind-body continuum in which others and the world become beloveds.

Barbara: Yes, beautiful!

Jean: Dante's closing words in *The Divine Comedy*: "*l'amor che muove il sol e l'altre stelle.*" The love that moves the sun and the other stars. And, you know, we ultimately come down to that. What is it about? It's about that apprehension of union, of connection, not just with one, but with the plurality of being—which then primes all further growth.

Barbara: This is the vision that has motivated me: the vision of being part of the body of humankind, and that body struggling to become one and moving towards the sense of universal life. It wasn't Barbara Hubbard connecting with God.

Hazel: Yes, I've always sensed that in you.

Barbara: And I don't think it's Hazel Henderson making just the personal link.

Hazel: Oh no.

Barbara: And you, Jean, wouldn't be working out in the world as you do, and at the New School for Social Research.

Jean: And with all of the little black children and prisoners.

Hazel: It's really the attempt to link the organic human species body.

Barbara: Maybe we've hit upon one of the key elements of feminine consciousness: putting that effort first.

Hazel: Yes!

Barbara: Each one of us could have pursued a life of deep contemplation. We could have become yogis. You probably are one, Jean, but you don't spend all of your time in a lotus position. You are out in the world.

Jean: Yogi means union.

Barbara: Yes, but in the traditional forms, yogis spent a great deal of time isolated from the world. You have a tremendously active life. And so does Hazel, and so do I. You, being a real worker in the spiritual field, are manifesting this sense externally.

Jean: This is the new form of Eros!

Barbara: I have a vision of you as seeing all of the members of the human species, and being attracted to the potential of each one. And the more that you can reach with your power to emancipate them, the more the human species will be able to connect. You have a very powerful motivation to reach a lot of people. How do you see that desire to reach as many as possible?

Jean: Well, it didn't begin that way. From about 1960 until about five years ago I had been working with thousands of individuals on a one-to-one basis. And then I began to realize that these things *could* happen—it works! And now I've gotten rid of a lot of the little local self—the galloping hubris and a certain arrogance that comes from having been too successful too early, and a college professor at nineteen. That's a lot of garbage! If you can get rid of that, the channels become much clearer. When you get rid of the unnecessary ego protections—leaving enough, of course, to keep body and mind and soul together, and to make you get up in the morning—then the flow to others becomes very natural. It's not a question of having to go out and reach more people; it's just that one is prepared, and the natural ecology of things demands it. But I'm glad I wasn't cut loose on the world fifteen years ago!

Barbara: But you're cut loose on the world now.

Jean: Yes, but in a condition I hope and pray is not ego conditioned. And it has to be cleaned out and revitalized every morning! Not for reasons of ego, but because of the accumulation of garbage—people projecting things on to you: angers; fears; hostilities. You know all about that.

Hazel: Yes, right.

Barbara: How do you clear out in the morning?

Jean: Well, there are many ways of doing it. I lie there, and my mind becomes a marvelous emptiness, and a great expanse. It's the breathing into that and realizing that I am no-thing . . . and that when being began nothing mattered. *[laughter]* But it needs constant observation. Any moment that I'm a little suspicious that I'm doing something for reasons that might be ambitious or personal—I stop.

Hazel: Isn't that interesting, Jean, the extension to the next level of the observer/observed thing. This is very important to me; I find that I'm constantly watching myself. If I find that I'm doing things hysterically, or for ego needs, or for any of the old motivations that I'm trying to shed, I want to monitor it and get rid of it. We've recreated the old dichotomy on the next level.

Jean: Yes, that's very interesting.

Barbara: I find that I do the same thing: constantly monitoring myself to see if my ego, my hubris, my desire to succeed, is what's motivating what I'm doing. The further I grow, the more my ego sticks out like a sore thumb—a painful anachronism that stops my growth. I have to get *it* out of *my* way!

Jean: You have to allow yourself moments of tremendous spontaneity. In the morning, when you are "morninged," the world is full, and you lose the little local self; the leaky margins allow you to become diaphanous to the rhythms of the universe. It's the great cleansing.

Barbara: Here's another aspect of the feminine principle.

Jean: It's a profound passivity. Not: "Watch out world, here I come!" Which is how many men view themselves in the morning! *[laughter]*

Barbara: All of us are effective women in the sense that we are out in the world doing things that do have effects. But we're checking ourselves; we're allowing our Higher Selves to monitor our activities to check for ego and hostility, and to clear out and relate to the whole each day. We are moving beyond self-oriented consciousness to holistic consciousness.

Hazel: The motive has to be right or the results could be disastrous. I've seen so much of that that I've become very, very aware.

One of the things that I'm now talking a great deal about is the need for a reflective science. Instead of the paradigm being "scientist observes phenomenon," you have to pull back one photo frame so that it becomes "scientist observing scientist observing phenomenon." Even though this has overtones of control, and we all get very upset about control, we must remember that voluntary control is really the essence of true freedom and of the next stage of growth. But you suggest, as I've been suggesting the last few years, that scientists should perhaps voluntarily submit themselves to psychoanalysis in order to understand their true motives.

Jean: Well, I don't know about psychoanalysis, but certainly some kind of analysis.

Hazel: Yes, some sort of reflection about why they're doing what they're doing. Gerald Holton, the physicist from Harvard, has been so wonderful in trying to develop that same kind of self-awareness. I think that that's about the only attitude that will make one's instrumental rationality really responsible and self-limiting. I have a fear of runaway positive feedback systems. If instrumental rationality just goes charging on without the self-limiting, cybernetic control, it becomes cancerous.

Barbara: The real joy in this—the "scientist observing scientist observing photon"—is that as the observer becomes more aware, the rewards and the pleasure increase dramatically.

Jean: Yes, because one becomes less self-conscious, and more Self-conscious. This is an ancient Buddhist exercise: the watcher of the watcher of the watcher. You watch yourself watching yourself watching yourself—and soon the whole thing begins to break down. It's a koan kind of thing. And it finally becomes just Self and photon. You *become* the great interdependent realm of being.

Barbara: And the reward of that is such tremendous fulfillment that the ego needs are lessened. I've had experiences like this, where the joy was so great that the idea of being worried about ego rewards was too paltry to even consider. I've had those moments of connection—that's what keeps me going. You would never need, for instance, a status reward, because it doesn't feel as good.

Hazel: And also, this whole idea of peer group recognition—when you realize how sorry a state the peer group is in, it can actually be a slap in the face!

Barbara: It can be a signal that you haven't gone very far!

Jean: But there are still moments in time when one needs a vital affirmation from the depths of one's being . . . quite apart from who and what you are.

Barbara: Yes, that's quite different. It's the need for *communion.*

Hazel: And there is another kind of vital affirmation, which is why I am enjoying being here at this very moment. At a time when there is a sense of this emergent consciousness, and we are trying to express it, and amplify it, and link it, and play midwife to it, we do need the psychic support of finding and affirming others who are doing the same thing, and to receive their affirmation. This is just vital to me; otherwise you tend to feel that you're operating on a rather esoteric wavelength.

Barbara: One of the things that I find I must constantly deal with is this question of—What have I accomplished? Usually, in looking back, it seems as if I really haven't accomplished anything at all—abortive attempt after abortive attempt. But I've begun to feel that maybe that's the wrong question.

Hazel: It is. You see, *you* are the accomplishment. We're so product oriented! You, as a being, are a very beautiful product. That's the accomplishment—you and your interactions.

Jean: Do you by any chance remember the film back in 1946 called *It's a Wonderful Life*? It begins with a guy falling off of a bridge. And suddenly someone else falls into the water beside him. It's this curious little being—an Irish drunken angel who says to him, "Now where did you want to go?" And he answers, "My life has been awful, shameful; I've accomplished nothing!" "Oh, you think so?" says the drunken angel. "Why don't we go back and see what the world would have been like if you hadn't lived!" And the whole town becomes a complete mess! *[laughter]* And so the drunken angel earns his wings for that one! But the point is true: one's life is the accomplishment. Why must one have a debit and credit list? That's the old Judeo-Christian programming.

Barbara: Well, let's take an example—the Salk vaccine. Now that's a wonderful accomplishment. It's wonderful that children don't get polio. If I were Jonas Salk, I could get up in the morning and say, "Never mind everything else, because of my work, children are no longer getting polio." Now that's an accomplishment; there are such things.

Jean: And who is not getting jaundice of the soul because you have been? And who may be *living* because of you?

Hazel: And who has been helped to grow by you? Me, for one.

Barbara: I'm not saying that the human being is not a wonderful product.

Jean: You're talking about acknowledgement.

Barbara: No, it has nothing to do with being acknowledged. In the case of Jonas, no matter what kind of person he might be, or anything else, he has achieved something very tangible.

Jean: But there are still other modes of creation that are less tangible, but no less significant.

Barbara: But you can't discount the more tangible kind of achievement.

Jean: No, you don't discount it, but you don't want to make it the only thing that dominates your consciousness. This is another thing about being female: the accomplishments are much more subtle.

Hazel: They are not quantifiable.

Jean: They are resonance achievements, not quantifiable achievements—by and large.

Hazel: I think that that is why the whole Eastern sort of approach has been so helpful to me; that is, looking at the fields of interplay rather than the entities. This has helped me to see that there is no way that a foundation could fund what I do. If you could quantify it, I probably wouldn't have bothered to do it in the first place. And so you have to understand that what we're doing is playing around with fields of interplay, and that there is no way for the dominant culture to reward that.

V

Are We Still Children Playing in Pandora's Box?

Networking. Self-organizing systems. Imaging: "an image is always a mythic form." A sustainable economy." On technology: technologies of transcendence; appropriate technologies. The disparity between the hardware and the necessary software. The critical viability test.

Hazel: Let's turn this idea of nonquantifiable achievements upside down for a minute—I do this all the time with the public interest groups I'm involved with. Whenever some sort of project comes up, everybody right away wants to get a million dollars to do this, and do that; and I say: "No, don't you understand that we have to stay below the poverty line? The moment this organization starts producing glossy annual reports on coated paper and all the rest of it . . ." That's the way that I measure other public interest groups to decide whether or not they've joined the devil! If they're getting enough money from the dominant culture to make those sorts of manifestations, they aren't doing anything new. It's always been my measure of what's going on in that world that's any good; it's got to be below the poverty line!

And of course the other thing is that that's a very organic sort of model; it's also a very sustainable sort of model. Once you start going 3-D with all of their tools, they can pull the plug on you. But if you're using your own psychic energies, and a very limited amount of material things, they don't even notice that you're there.

Jean: Using third- and fourth-world meta-technologies you can change a world.

Hazel: That's right!

Jean: But if you use the devil tools, you merely become a denizen of hell.

Hazel: And there's all this beautiful, yeasty stuff going on, fermenting just below the surface—and it's beneath contempt! The dominant culture doesn't believe it, and that's its advantage.

Barbara: Like Christ—he wasn't even noticed.

Jean: But they didn't even have a plan?

Hazel: No. It's called the muddling-through mode. But this may actually come to their rescue because there is a lot of very life-oriented stuff going on there. The people have realized that the government is an abstraction and that they had better do it themselves.

Barbara: Hazel, in managing the decline of the industrial society, what do you see us managing ourselves toward?

Hazel: Basically toward what I'm calling the emerging countereconomy, which is, for example, these fifty million Americans who are already participating in some form of cooperative enterprise. All it is is a reconfiguration of the modes of production and distribution. It's just like ancient Rome, where all of the transportation lines got too extenuated.

It doesn't mean to say that people will no longer be provisioned, and that there will be no more innovation. All that will still go on. It's just that the palaces will crumble, and the overgrowth of centralized structures will devolve. What's so interesting is that the most irrelevant places in the world right now are Washington, London, Paris, New York, Canberra. The nation-state control level is being superceded on the global level, and pulled back to reality on the local level.

Jean: There are no great central places anymore!

Barbara: You could see it happening with Jimmy Carter, who looked very powerful until he got to Washington. And suddenly, it's almost as though the complexities are diminishing him. He looks less and less powerful as he settles into the White House. I call it the "principle of rising impotence." The higher you go, the more structured-in you become. You are forced to maintain the existing system rather than evolve it.

Hazel: Because you are climbing into a dead coral reef! The life has migrated out of it.

Jean: Carter's great claim to the presidency was that he did not know the coral reef, and that he would bring fresh life.

Barbara: But he's ended up appointing denizens of the old coral reef to his cabinet!

Hazel: There is such a basic contradiction there. And then there was the rationalization that, "Well, we'll have all the new voices in the undersecretaryships." I've been asked several times what role I would play. They wanted me to be a member of the transition group and all of that. I've been saying an emphatic no! I'm not going to climb onto the dead coral reef and tie my hands behind my back.

Basically, the question is: Can it slide down gracefully without hurting too many? But it isn't really a decline! The life is all going somewhere else; it's migrating.

Jean: You know, every era has its dominant forms. We're moving now from Homo-politicus and Homo-economicus to . . . where? Maybe it's back to Homo-religiosis in the root meaning—"religio," meaning "to bind."

Barbara: Union; to bind back together.

Jean: Back together, and back into the cosmos.

Hazel: Again, it's this molecule-making image that had been forgotten when we got into the all-looking-at-the-dictator mode. Now we're finally going back to learning how to nucleate, to self-organize.

Jean: The power is moving to the countermodels.

Hazel: It certainly isn't Washington, which inhabited largely by Neanderthals.

Jean: No, not even Neanderthals! If they were Neanderthals they would at least be sensitive, but they're not; they're pterodactyls! But smart pterodactyls!

Hazel: Oh yes, they're not dumb.

Jean: But are they really as bad as the impression I got from my experience down there?

Hazel: Well, maybe yours was pretty bad, but I think it's generally true.

Jean: Does that mean that to become a member of Congress is automatically to—

Hazel: Well, look at the experience you have to go through to become a member of Congress. You've got to lie; you've got to deny your inner nature; you've got to be infatuated with power.

Jean: The education of a brontosaurus!

Hazel: Richard Nixon was the manifestation of the process you have to go through in order to become president. The problem is that anyone with a reasonably evolved consciousness has to wonder if they can put themselves into a pterodactyl suit!

[laughter]

Hazel: The networking that's going on between social-change people right now . . . thank God the people in Washington don't know about it! There was a conference on networking in Canada recently that I was invited to, but I was very suspicious about it. It was a bunch of typical academic hucksters—I thought, with my orientation—and they were going to impale this phenomenon: networking! And they were going to map it, and they were going to give it form, and go to the National Science Foundation and get grants. The people who network were going to be guinea pigs; they were going to eavesdrop on the network.

However, the beautiful thing about social-change networking is that they can't do that; all you have to do is regroup, change the name of the group, alter the telephone numbers, and go on as before. But they were going to intercept the chain of command, find out who the leaders are, find out the location where all of the subversive activity is going on . . . It's wonderful! They've got all the wrong images! Besides, there's really a subversive in every family: it's either the wife or the children. There is no chain of command; it's all autonomously self-actualizing human beings with the same image in their heads. It's self-organizing activity.

The metaphor that I think is important for the kind of culture that's emerging from this Logos is the metaphor of self-organization. We know that we're self-organizing systems. We know many instances of human culture that have been self-organizing, and that have had magnificently complex structures of behavior mediation and regulation, and that have been in perfect balance with their ecosystems. So we have all of those models of self-organization. All we don't know how to do—and maybe we never will—is to organize ourselves with this level of what Jean would call prosthetic types of technology. Not that we want to throw away the knowledge stock, or degrade it, but we do want to assert our own innate ability to self-organize, and to redress that imbalance.

One example of this is that we do want to restore the balance in regulating human behavior. If you have viable psychic structures of sanctions, regulations, and ways of mediating behavior, you don't need whips, guns, prisons, police forces, and all the rest of it.

Jean: And chemical determinants of consciousness.

Hazel: Right! You don't need any of those things. But at the same time we don't want to go back and totally recreate the so-called primitive way of regulating societies, because they might have had to lay a tremendously heavy trip on the children of that culture in order to do it.

Jean: Yes—an enormous insularity of the society.

Hazel: But we could do it in a voluntary way by imaging holographic images of society, by imaging on the next level that innate ability to self-organize. This is the whole metaphor of self-management. There are two metaphors of industrial societies at the moment that are terribly pregnant: worker or citizen participation, and self-management.

Jean: But you can not manage while you're still being educated for the year 1825, which is what our education prepares us for.

Hazel: Yes, so if we could be released from the old kinds of images, and go back to our own innate, intuitive wisdom that allows us to self-manage ourselves, and our familial interactions, we can also begin to self-manage at an institutional level. But this will require the development of a lot of very potent images, if you can have enough people aligning themselves around those images . . .

Jean: Well, we know that growth only occurs in terms of some kind of image of what it means to be human. The problem of our time is that the old images have run out.

Hazel: But they're emerging; we can see bits and pieces of the new images beginning to emerge.

Hazel: They are emerging in science fiction; they are emerging in new myth. Whenever you want to examine what's emerging in the mindscape, look at the new mythic images.

Barbara: But what if you're looking for a new image of a person? I don't have that at all clear.

Hazel: Of a person?

Barbara: Of a person after whom I could be modeling myself.

Jean: Nor should you! An image is always a mythic form; a myth is something that never was but is always happening. Both of you have very precise, inchoate longings for what it is!

Hazel: That we do! *[laughter]*

Jean: We're modeling in images, you see. The problem today is that so many young people don't have images. Television may be wiping out, on neurological levels, a lot of their image-making capacity—little strobes pulsing in front of them for five hours a day from the time they are two years old. Thus the images of the future tend to come from older people. This is not good; I think, however, that it can be redressed.

But there is nothing so powerful as an image whose time has come, spelled out with great gutsy, visceral language! And in music, and in painting. That can do more to sweep away the anachronisms than anything that we could do in our pushing against the mountain.

Hazel: Of all that intellectual paraphernalia!

Jean: One of the things that we should keep in mind is: What are the images of the possible as we see it? Perhaps we should even try to do a little image building—in terms of person, process, and social form.

Hazel: Well, I'd like to throw in one image here. I've just done a paper for the AAAS, for a day-long panel they're having on economic growth—all of the old images, of course. So I've done this paper that I've called "The Emerging Countereconomy." I am simply saying that there are the green shoots of a new type of economy, technology, lifestyle, and way of being emerging right now, but that none of our machinery in Washington can even conceptualize it. And so they're not tracking it. And, as in any other dying culture, the very indicators of the well-being of the culture are hooked to the well-being of the dominant institutions. Naturally it will look as if the culture is all going to hell—if measured by those kinds of indicators.

I've started this paper with a paragraph I came across in a recently published book called *The Promise of the Coming Dark Age.* It was so useful in terms of turning the whole thing around and saying: "Let's look for a countereconomy statistically." My paper is essentially a plea to all of these clever institutionalized people who have computers, which I don't have, to go and hang some data of some of these new growth points. And I found a few little figures to spur them on: first of all, that fifty million people today participate in co-ops! Fifty million Americans! So there is a place to start that says something very, very new about what's going on. And then there are statistics indicating that the small family farm is more efficient than the agra-business farm ten times its size! And the fact that transportation is no longer a free good, meaning that regional and local distribution and exchange systems are now more efficient than nationwide ones. So let's start making some statistics that will monitor that.

Barbara: Hazel, in talking about new technologies, how would you evaluate the next generation of technologies that would include such things as the satellite for education over India, which is producing on a miniaturized basis an enormous amount of information, and then the weather-monitoring satellites, and so forth?

Hazel: Well, I don't want to say a total no to all of these things, but I am suggesting that we no longer have the wisdom to use all of those sorts of things.

Barbara: We no longer have—?

Hazel: Or we've lost it, to use Jean's kind of imagery. For example, I read a report on that Indian educational satellite system; you know what has happened to that, don't you?

Barbara: No.

Hazel: Well, it's become purely a propaganda tool; it's absolutely nothing but thought control. It's a totalitarian state going into every village. And the fascinating thing is that they have found that if you go to some of these little Indian villages, the television sets are on all the time. They fiddle with the channels to snow up the screen, and it creates light! They don't have electric light by which to see in the evenings, so they can then sit around and talk by the light of the flashing television set! It's wonderful! *[laughter]* You see, we don't have the wisdom to use all of that stuff. We're still children playing around in Pandora's box. That is not the growth point.

Barbara: Well, we certainly can't stay at this level of technology, which might, as you say, be destructive. But it's just an early form. I believe that technology is natural. There is a technological aspect to everything on the material plane. And there is an evolving continuum of technologies throughout the evolutionary transcendence—tools that will produce a quantum leap—as the genetic code technology produced a quantum leap from the large molecules. Technologies like astronautics, cybernetics, genetics, and so on, will make it possible for humans to transcend the mammalian condition physically— brutalizing work, certain kinds of disease, planet-boundness. We are at an early phase of *human* technological development, but not of technology itself. That has been going on since the origin of the physical universe. I believe that as we begin to understand synergy and whole systems both on Earth and in space our technologies will improve enormously. They will be ephemeralized, as Bucky Fuller says—more biological than mechanical.

Hazel: Yes, of course, I didn't mean to make a blanket statement. There are many technologies that are already appropriate—tape recorders are a very appropriate sort of technology; they're individual; they allow personal control. A typewriter is a very appropriate technology, a sewing machine, power tools …

Jean: But here we have to ask: Appropriate to what? If we begin to define the emerging image of what it means to be human, and the larger notion of life and its capacities, then you begin to discover those technologies that are appropriate.

Hazel: Well, what I mean, I think, is those technologies that are appropriate to our level of wisdom.

Jean: Yes! But if you can extend that level of wisdom—

Hazel: Then you can do all of these other things.

Jean: Not necessarily.

Hazel: You may not want to!

Jean: You may not want to; you may have a totally different kind of technology.

Hazel: One of the ideas that fascinates me right now is this idea of the road not taken. In the field of energy, for example: We went the Edison route to electricity, but apparently there was an entirely different conceptualization of how to get electricity that was conceived of by Nikola Tesla that was relegated to the dust bin of history. If we had gone the Tesla route, we might not have any huge power stations; his was a much simpler conceptualization.

Jean: This is where you need Jay Forrester's kind of model—to take the Tesla route and see what would be the playout in terms of the whole socio-economic structure.

Hazel: Well, we certainly could have a crack at it, and use it as an intellectual device.

Barbara: We've been talking about this enormous potential of the human brain, and we know that potentially we have the wisdom to do a tremendous number of things. It seems to me that these developing technologies, many of which may be inappropriate, are just a prelude. They are the products of the human intelligence manifesting itself in new prosthetic bodies, many forms of which be viable. Where I really disagree with you, Hazel, is that I think that these new capacities may be essential in terms of our corporate wisdom, and our corporate connections. We are, after all, becoming a globally interdependent society.

Hazel: They may be.

Barbara: And these things are coming along modestly, as they should.

Hazel: But the point is that they're already ahead of us. It's this idea of cultural lag: We're always better at creating the hardware than we are at writing the program of software that we need to make it work for us. For instance, we've created an interdependent world economy basically through technological interlinkage. And now we're desperately trying to write the program of software to make it work: the monetary agreements, the political agreements, and all of that. We always seem to be about ten years behind in writing the software—sometimes a lot further.

Jean: Wait a minute; wait a minute! This is very interesting. You're saying that the subjective part of the human experience is running ten years behind the objective. Man the bridges; devil take the hindmost! Just do it, and then see what happens—which is typical frontier psychology. But we've come to the end of the frontier age. I think that what we're seeing here, and this is part of the rise of the feminine principle in our time, is a reversal in which the subjective *techné*—meaning skill, not technology—is ten years ahead of objectification. It's a reality-quake that is happening in many people, especially young people: people making almost unimaginable leaps in being so that they're no longer living in the same universe as their parents. It's not really a generation gap; it's a reality gap, which is much more serious.

What we have here is two separate realities running in tandem: one on which, in terms of technological process, the objectification is way ahead of subjectification. Software. And simultaneously there is this reality-quake in which the experience of forms of consciousness, of ways of being, is running way ahead of the objective hardware. Now how do we bring those two things together?

Barbara: That's very interesting, because both are certainly true.

Hazel: And so really it's a bringing into time-phase from two different directions.

Jean: Yes!

Barbara: But in many cases the hardware is actually forcing the software. The most extreme example, of course, is the atomic bomb. The Third World War is unthinkable, so we are forced to find new modes of dealing with conflict.

Hazel: Well, Charles de Gaulle called the atom bomb "the prince of peace." I see this whole nuclear thing as a forcing function, but the stakes are extremely high, and the outcome is uncertain. I mean, we could self-destruct very easily.

A very nice demonstration of that idea has to do with Carl Sagan, who has been very interested in finding life in other places in the universe. As I understand it, when he was doing a computer analysis on the probability of finding life in the universe, he had to program into his computer the probability that an enormous number of life-bearing planets that might have evolved to this technological fifth stage would just self-destruct.

Barbara: I think that's very likely.

Hazel: Yes, that sounds very realistic to me.

Barbara: I think that in that sense we may be going through a last judgment on this phase of life. If we don't succeed in coordinating the hardware with the software, the subjective with the objective, we won't make it, as a species, to the next phase.

Hazel: Or we may recycle and have another crack at it.

Barbara: Yes, but this time around we are going through a very critical viability test. This is why I have such a sense of urgency.

Jean: What do you mean by recycling, Hazel? We've already run through the resources!

Hazel: Well, you can imagine all sorts of tectonic plate activity that could reconstitute the resources. A very imaginative Yugoslavian friend of mine was doing a paper on ancient civilizations. In Yugoslavia, you see, the scientific tradition is very free and you're allowed to hypothesize all sorts of wild things. My friend had been hypothesizing about much earlier cultures, and the whole lost Atlantis theme. And he was saying that there is absolutely no scientific way that we can be sure that these things are fables, because tectonic plate activity could mean that even a culture that had developed as much concrete and steel as ours could be completely reconstituted. Even New York City, if it were to slip under a tectonic plate, would be reconstituted very rapidly. So recycling at that level is perfectly possible. A million years from now all the resources would again be available.

Barbara: It seems unlikely to me that a human species would evolve a second time on this planet; however, it doesn't really matter. There are probably billions of planets with experiments of life. If we don't make it through this phase, there will be other experiments of life in the universe that do. But I have the feeling that although we may be immature as a species, we have the potential and will succeed. The intelligence of fifteen billion years of evolution is working with us.

We have the potential

VI

Women Reconceiving the World!

*The critical nexus of human history. The emergence
of feminine principles: a survival response. An expanded
maternal energy. Making the world work/getting
the thing done! The Earth as embryo: the metaphor of gestation.
"We are thrusting against the womb, and the midwives are ready."*

Barbara: I think that part of this urgency that we all feel, if it's at all legitimate, has to do with this sense that the connecting and coordinating functions on this planet are occurring very rapidly. It's perhaps comparable to a certain moment in the process of birth. We have to learn to handle our environmental crises; we have to learn to stop polluting our habitat; we have to learn to identify with all of humanity and not to have nuclear conflict. These are all new skills.

Jean: In terms of the known history of the human race, we are at the most critical nexus for survival or death of the species. And we are also at the threshold of a richer and more extended mode of being than the human race has ever known. We are living right now in that critical time phase. It's probably a fifty-year period—maybe less.

Barbara: I sense that myself. What are the elements of that criticality, Jean, as you sense it?

Jean: Well, I think we've been talking about that criticality all day. We've been talking about the great disparity between the objectification of the world and the subjective factors that will allow us to orchestrate that objectification. And then there is the critical density of global interdependence—this is frightening! I cannot cough without there being repercussions at great distances; this is a metaphor, of course, but the point is true.

We've never before had a globally interdependent society. We have never had societies in which the ecology of things has become so thick that there is no innocence anywhere. And that is probably the most frightening thing of all. I mean, what General Motors may do does make a difference. What I think does make a difference. We needn't talk anymore about having to convince the higher-ups; the density is such that it has radically democratized the difference between higher-ups and lower-downs. What you do can make as much difference to the saving of a planet as anything anybody else can do—be it President Carter or MacGeorge Bundy, the head of the Ford Foundation. My old friend John Platt, who has done some writing on hierarchical structuring—

Hazel: Step function.

Jean: Step function, yes. As he points out, when you get to critical density, one little quantum change, and suddenly—the entire structure falls! The French Revolution: the work of centuries was overthrown in months!

In six thousand years of known history we have never known a situation like this. It's probably more like seven thousand years. And it's probably safe to say one hundred thousand years before that. We can no longer say: "Oh, nothing new under the sun; I'm just gonna sit like a bump on a log." There is no way that we can do that! We are at the critical nexus of this historical time!

Hazel: I think we all sense that, and that's what gives us the sense of urgency, and our different ways of expressing the energy overdrive. I think that this sense of urgency really is a survival thing—it has nothing to do with ego in the male sense.

Jean: Well, this is why the female principle is rising! It's a reality arising in time. The male ego as structured in this time is not sufficient to be able to deal with these kinds of things!

Barbara: It's a maternal urgency.

Jean: Yes! A maternal urgency and a great blowout in receptivity that you find in feminine function as it has been structured.

Barbara: I'd like to add a little anecdote that relates to this. This past Christmas I had all of my daughters at home with me—they're all wonderful. My youngest daughter, Alex, had brought home with her a book about whales, and my daughter Stephanie, who had never thought a bit about whales in her whole life, started to read this book. And immediately she became passionately outraged—"This is just horrible what they're doing to the baby whales! How can the human species—!" She was apoplectic! And I began to think about maternal energy: she was acting like a mother would act if someone were coming in and killing her children!

Jean: It's a mode of identification.

Barbara: She was identifying with the baby whales! It's as if they were a part of her. And of course they're having these marvelous whale festivals in California now that Alex goes to and tells me about. The young people, not just women, are really concerned about the whales. A few years ago it didn't bother anybody. I see this as a generalized maternal energy beginning to manifest itself in terms of the whole. But the passion involved is what really impressed me.

Hazel: And it's so beautiful, because really the identification with that particular creature is quite illogical—so many other chains in the ecosystem are being ripped apart. Yet, at the emotional level, it doesn't really matter: the whale is a metaphor for all creature consciousness.

Barbara: I think we are beginning to see, then, that this maternal urgency is manifesting in a way that's very different than masculine urgency—which would be to dominate, manipulate, and control.

Jean: To get the thing done!

Hazel: That's right. And to get it done efficiently!

Jean: This, on the other hand, is a way of making things work. There is an enormous difference between making the world work and getting things done. And that is the great dichotomy.

Hazel: And even worse is the mode of getting things done efficiently.

That is the most bankrupt—

Jean: Cost-benefit analysis! *[laughter]*

Hazel: The most bankrupt possible way of doing anything! But, you know, my friend Eugene Odum, the ecologist, drew something very interesting to my attention when I was talking about the way human consciousness now is identifying with animal consciousness. It's this idea of ecosystems as immanent information. This, of course, is what I'm trying to say when I say that only the system can manage the system, and that only the system can model the system. But there was an article in *Science* magazine back in 1968, I believe, about grasslands; grasslands, it seems, can grow themselves tougher, and more unpalatable, by increasing the cellulose in their leaves if there are too many grazing animals. So they can literally send away some of the animals. Now at that level of identifying with the mother planet, and of identifying with the idea of "Gaia"—which is James Lovelock's and Lynn Margulies' idea of the whole biosphere as one organism . . .

Jean: Which is probably conscious! Those grasslands, in growing themselves tougher, probably did it to some extent as conscious intent. This is very different than our notion of conscious intent, of course. And the planet itself may be doing this, too—there has been an incredible intensification of earthquakes and natural disasters in recent years.

Barbara: And not just the planet—the solar system is probably doing it too. When I identify with nature, it's much broader than just the planet. When I see the moon, I feel intimately related to it, and also to the sun, and to the other planets. I think that that is where I differ from you: my environment is intuitively the universe. I feel this identification with the Earth, but I feel in no way restricted to that body. It's a feeling so deep inside of me that I have to take it seriously. My environment is not just this planet.

Hazel: But your physical being is made up of the elements of this planet.

Jean: But also of the elements of the sun.

Barbara: And of the stars!

Jean: You are already a cosmic jet-setter in terms of your substance and organization.

Barbara: And that's why I believe that it is completely natural for us to consciously partake of the cosmos, physically as well as consciously.

Hazel: We are the children of second-generation stars.

Barbara: But I'm not just speaking metaphysically; I'm speaking of the maturation of the species—our physical environment will not just be this planet. I believe that we will in time be living beyond this planet. The resources of our solar system are as much our body as our Earth. But without the feminine principle, this could unleash a deadly power. I am completely in tune with what we've been talking about here, except that I believe that maternal consciousness can aid in expanding human consciousness physically as well as consciously into the cosmos.

Jean: Let's play around with an image for a moment. Take the Earth as a central point—an embryo. Take the spheres, the planets, as the surrounding womb; the sun perhaps as mother . . . and the surrounding spaces as the amniotic fluid. And the sun was born of another mother. . . . Now use that metaphor of gestation. . . . What do you do with it?

Hazel: What happens, in other words, when the Earth baby emerges?

Jean: Or . . . it doesn't even have to be emerging. What are the modes of quickening in the womb?

Barbara: Well, many things happen. First of all, in thinking of birth, the contact with the mother—the sun—begins to deepen: the fetus begins to know that intimate source of nourishment, and to understand how to make use of that vital solar energy. It begins to know the language and the intelligence of the sun, and begins to communicate with that intelligence. I've always been struck by the fact that in the beginning a newborn baby doesn't know it has a mother; but when the nervous system becomes more connected, then it begins to interact with the mother. So, taking this image, as we begin to go through this critical phase of interlinkage and interaction, I think we will begin to know our mother, the sun, in terms of its energy and intelligence. We, too, if we're a child in this image, will grow to become mothers to other children. We're infantile at this point, but we will grow to become cocreative. We are even beginning to conceive of reproducing "Gaia"—our Earth and biosphere—in the space colonies.

Jean: And all those UFOs are just a bunch of women! *[laughter]* A Martian Hadassah! *[great peals of laughter]*

Hazel: I love it! How wicked! *[laughter continues and gradually subsides]*

Barbara: You've interrupted my reverie!

Jean: Okay, let's go back to the image. As the baby in the womb is fed by the placenta, so we are fed from within the Earth itself. Now, as we begin to extend that image, and become a cosmic species . . .

Barbara: We begin to be nourished directly by solar energy.

Jean: The mother's breast.

Barbara: Eventually, as we continue to mature, we will be able to leave the mother's breast and extract energy for ourselves from the larger environment— the cosmos. We will become cocreators. I think that as a species we are now at the infantile stage in terms of our potential, though some individuals are beginning to have a sense of that potential. But—as with the development of a baby—none of the vital stages can be skipped. Our minds may be able to project, but we as a body have to grow; we have to acquire the skills and wisdom that will be necessary to fulfill this vision. If any one of the critical stages is bypassed, we could simply be wiped out.

Jean: Although individuals may succeed in achieving this vital sense, and become "like unto gods" as all the scriptures tell us, it must happen to us as a whole. We are at this critical nexus, and we are either dying, or we are joining a much larger universe. And also, a much larger universe is joining us.

And that is important: otherwise we think we have to lift ourselves up into the cosmos by our own bootstraps, and that's the wrong image. This is the priming! We are thrusting against the womb, and the midwives are ready.

VII

Metaphysical Balls

Brain function: Brain does not secrete mind. Cosmic or Christic Consciousness. The physics of envisioning: Everything begins in vision. Reality is as we construct it! Devolution and decentralization. "Union differentiates."

Barbara: Jean, I would like to ask you a question about the evolution of the human brain. Is it possible that there is something happening to the brain in terms of evolutionary change?

Jean: Well, fourteen quadrillion things are happening in the brain at any given instant.

Barbara: Yes, but I'm wondering about the evolution of consciousness. Could there be some kind of evolutionary chance that might be leading towards something like cosmic consciousness? I don't know, really, whether I'm talking about an actual physiological change in the brain, or whether it's something far more simple—a response to new stimuli perhaps.

Jean: That's a difficult question to answer directly, but let's talk for a moment about what we know about the brain. First of all, have you ever watched closely the movements of a very small child? A normal three-year-old, for instance, is almost constantly engaged in some form of body movement—dancing around, swinging an arm or a leg . . . Now, if you take a Harvard fullback, and ask him to follow and imitate all the movements of a three-year-old, he will literally collapse after two hours and have to go to bed for a week. This is why a child is able to learn so much so quickly. There is so much stimulation, and so many connections being made in the brain, that a child is a regular osmosis machine for processing information. With the stopping of movement comes the stopping of brain function.

Now, it has been theorized that the brain is unfinished. There are three sections of the human brain, and parts of these sections are really not very well connected. The oldest part of the brain is not very well connected to the newest part. If you are really interested in the evolution of your own brain, you can, through certain exercises, actually being to put down pathways and being to establish these connections.

With regard to the idea of cosmic consciousness, some recent research suggests that when you are meditating, and you begin to get into the one-seven-one cycle—which is the cycle of the Earth as well—then quantum tunneling occurs between all of the cells. If you are meditating, let's say, in certain cellular areas, then a generalization occurs—these cells trigger millions of other cells, which in turn trigger millions of other cells, so that you have whole area of the brain in this pulse. And this pulse is a great quieting. It is thought that this great pulsing of the whole brain relates to an innate matrix of stillness, and that this stillness may then relate, ecologically, probably through field phenomena, to other areas of being, or to the larger ecology of things—

what you might call cosmic consciousness. So, you see, the doorways are already physiologically structured in the brain.

Now, at the same time, two leading brain physiologists—Wilder Penfield and Sir John Eccles—conclude, after lifetimes of study, that *mind is ultimately separate from brain*. Mind uses brain as a kind of bio-computer; it is prior to brain, and gives brain its designs. Brain does *not* secrete mind!

Barbara: Mind would then be a disembodied energy?

Jean: We don't know, but it uses brain as matrix.

Barbara: Could the mind be synonymous with what has usually been called soul?

Jean: Well, we don't know. Probably there are layers and layers to the self. You find this notion in many ancient traditions; in ancient Egyptian tradition, for example, there are five or six levels of the self.

Barbara: You find this idea also in Bucke's *Cosmic Consciousness*.[3] It's Teilhardian, too, of course. Bucke talks about the idea that the founders of many of the great religious traditions—Christ, Buddha, and so—represented a new form of consciousness for the species that would eventually become common, just as at some point self-consciousness became a common reality. Christic consciousness, according to Bucke, is a highly evolved form that eventually all living humans will have. We're moving toward that form of consciousness.

Jean: A growing number of individuals in our time are moving towards that.

Barbara: Yes, and I'm wondering what that phenomenon is, because that really may be the salvation of the Earth. The number of individuals that can move towards that form of consciousness could make the difference in a critical period such as the one we're in.

Jean: Out of ecological necessity! It may be necessity entering into time. It's a kind of cooperative consciousness, the first levels of which may not appear in mystical or even in psychological terms. The first level may be manifesting itself in terms of fifty million Americans participating in co-ops. They may be the first manifest, objective form of what is happening as a subjective event—what you would call Christic consciousness.

Hazel: It's probably some kind of body wisdom.

Jean: And I think that you can engender it. It doesn't have to be engendered as meditation; it can probably happen in a simple co-op store. That already creates a level of communion and community that in turn will begin to encourage deeper levels. And you can approach it from any place—interior or objective. We are *Unus Mundus*: we are one world within and without, and so it doesn't matter where you start. I start from within because that's the nature of my job. You start from without—that's your mode.

Hazel: Yes, that's so true. It doesn't really matter where you start, or where you feel that you're best suited to making a contribution.

Jean: Suppose you enter into some very powerful, cooperative, communal event where you feel this sense of community, of love . . . Now what is happening to you psychologically in terms of the new brain theory? You begin, in terms of your brain, to resonate in a different kind of frequency. You don't have to be directing the action anymore—something takes over. It's a form of meditation—daily life as spiritual exercise. Any moment can be a loaded moment in which this frequency can begin to occur. It is a latent frequency that relates to the frequency of the Earth, and that ties you to the larger community, and to the community of the Earth itself. You become what in your terms would be cosmic or Christic being.

Barbara: This happened at SYNCONs when the walls began to come down and people started moving together—moving around together, dancing together, singing together. If there had been a psychic measure the "temperature" would have gone up. It was like being drawn together by some greater force. Unfortunately it was always lost when it was all over and we had to separate, but this memory is never lost.

Hazel: Let's talk for a moment about vision, which I think relates very closely to this movement towards cosmic consciousness we've been discussing. One of the things which I have learned in my own life, is that certain things are essential if one is to become part of the new being. One must have, first of all, the intuition, and the faith, that is a vision—even if you haven't yet any clearly defined sense of that vision. Faith is very important; you can't give up on that vision, even if it is vague. . . . I have always had that faith. And even if everyone around doubted it, it was real, it emerged. I have always had trust in the very deep levels of the vision.

Jean: And even if unseen, these things are real. They are there in their loaded, coded potencies.

Hazel: And we know how these unseen visions manifest themselves in very concrete ways.

Jean: Everything beings in vision. Would you like to know something about the physics of envisioning? It's quite interesting.

Hazel: Yes! That would be interesting.

Jean: Well, suppose you have something held very vividly as an image, or as a feeling—it can be touched, smelled, tasted . . . Somehow this switches on to the autonomic system, which is a very deep system relating to older areas of the brain. We have reason to believe that the autonomic system, when it is activated by images, is related to the bioplasmic fields that surround the body.

Hazel: Biosplasmic fields?

Jean: The electromagnetic fields surrounding the body. The image thus held sets up a wave frequency into the fields surrounding the body. This then, since we are ecosystems within ecosystems, envelopes within envelopes, sets up a wave system in other ecologies that are around us. In point of fact you do, quite concretely and quite physically, send images out into the atmosphere.

So, be careful of what you really want, because you're likely to get it. In other words, there is an ecology of happening—of how things happen. Your system sets up an imaginal wave that changes the electron balance, which changes other electron balances, and it begins on microcosmic levels to be encoded into the environment—so that what you really wish beings to occur.

Now, there are people who are able to sustain this, and they are the great optimists of the world—like Margaret Mead, for instance. Margaret gets almost everything she wants—because she is sure that reality would not *dare* to do otherwise! *[laughter]* Her reality is one of intense imagery: any event she sees, touches, hears, feels, smells. She feels it absolutely; she sends it out; she talks about it; and it begins to cohere. A deeply held thought, feeling, or image is literally a seed planted in the fields that surround us.

Barbara: So there is then a physiological basis for the envisioning process.

Jean: Yes. There are a lot of steps that we don't know, but the oscillation wave function of the autonomic system with respect to deeply held image is certainly part of it.

Hazel: Is there some kind of a theory that might be analogous to critical mass? Step theory? In other words, if enough people are imaging the same thing powerfully enough, and resonating, you do create the manifestation of that image.

Jean: Oh sure. There are many instances of this. Have you ever heard, for example, the story of rather queer group of thinkers in Britain who collectively projected the image of Rudolf Hess coming over to England? They did this for months: "Rudolf Hess, come over! Rudolf Hess, come over!" And for no particular reason Rudolf Hess got on a plane one day and flew over!

Hazel: No, I'd never heard that. Is it true?

Jean: Oh yes! Yes! They did it for months! And they actually brought him over. So, if you have a group of people that begins to work together—I mean a prayer circle is that kind of thing. Very frequently people are cured after prayer circles. Not the usual Christian prayer circle—"Oh, dear Lord, please!"—because then you're missing your step function. It's a level of affirmation, and the perception of a different reality.

Reality is as we construct it! There is a wonderful science fiction story—a John Collier story—that brings this idea home. It seems that a commuter train was pulling out of Paddington Station, and it leaped the track. And suddenly—*wham!*—it seemed to be back on the track again. And you see all the gentlemen in the first-class section reading their London *Times*. But the train starts going down—for hours and hours. "I say!" says one of the gentlemen, "we seem to have had a bit of a drop." And he goes on reading his London *Times*. But the train keeps hurtling downward. Eventually smoke begins to fill the compartment; fire is all around them. Finally, the train comes to a stop and they all get out. And here come all these curious little red men with long tails and pitchforks: "Get your burn cream here! Four shillings for burn cream!" "Get away from me, you filthy little man!" says one of the gentlemen. But he continues to make such a pest of himself that finally one rather dandy-looking young man says to him: "Do you know what? I don't believe in you!" "What did you say, sir?" says this repugnant little creature. "You beastly little thing, I don't believe in you!" "Oh, don't say that, sir!" "You beastly little thing, I *don't* believe in you!" And all of a sudden they find themselves back on the train, pulling into the station as usual. The next scene shows this same young man standing in front of the Bank of England shaking his fist and saying: "I don't believe in you!" *[laughter]*

But reality, in a curious way, is really like that! We are not innocent observers of the environment. One person can become a critical mass. It's better if there are more, of course. But a powerful imagizer—like Margaret Mead, who has no doubt about the effectiveness of her thought on the environment—gets about ninety percent return. It's a kind of metaphysical chutzpah that you have to have.

Hazel: But, you know, that image of standing in front of the Bank of England saying, "I don't believe in you!" and seeing the building begin to crack apart. That's the image of the imperial system right now.

Jean: Yes. That's what's happening. It's the people in the lower hierarchical levels who are saying "I don't believe!" and it *is* happening.

Hazel: Well, that's what devolution is all about. You see this in Britain. The word devolution is a very popular term in Britain right now, and also in Canada—and after the Yukon Indians, and Quebecois decided that they wanted to secede. This whole paradigm of devolution is very much on the minds of people in both of these countries.

And it's really interesting—I was talking recently to the British minister of technology. He sees citizen participation as devolution. In this country, if you mention devolution to an administrator or a corporate executive, they are absolutely terrified, and have this image of the whole thing sliding down; whereas in Britain and Canada devolution is seen in terms of the empowerment of citizen participation.

Barbara: So it's a different concept.

Hazel: Totally different. But it's the same effect! The reason you're having devolution in Britain, the reason the Welsh and the Scots are doing this independence thing, is because London can't do anything for them anymore. In other words, they're saying, "We don't believe in you." And the Quebecois are saying to Ottawa, "You're not mapping our reality anymore; we don't believe in you!"

Barbara: You know, Teilhard uses an interesting phrase that I think may describe this phenomenon: "Union differentiates." Now, if we are moving towards a planetary unity on one level, at the very same time a differentiation is occurring.

Hazel: And it must!

Jean: And you move into very interesting mixtures of human scale and human difference.

Barbara: Yes, and so the paradox is resolved if it is true that union differentiates. We can become more and more interconnected, while at the same time differentiating. Teilhard also goes on to say that as individuals, or cluster of individuals, enter freely into the whole, they become more and more uniquely themselves. I would use the word *evolution* rather than *devolution* for this phenomenon. Centralized systems have become overly complex and unmanageable. Out of their breakdown, a higher order is breaking through; a decentralization and differentiation of the parts into self-organizing units—with concurrent increase of interconnectedness and communications among the parts. We are evolving toward a more complex whole system—a synergistic whole—that will be greater than the sum of the parts.

Hazel: I love Dennis Livingston's image of a planet of neighborhoods.

Jean: Yes, very good.

Hazel: You see, what I am trying to say is that the only level of human organization that is truly irrelevant today is the nation-state and capital city. That is really part of the problem—that we're measuring the well-being of all these cultures in terms of the capital city and the nation-state.

Jean: Which are based on anachronistic modes of territorial imperatives!

Hazel: Yes! And we need so much above the nation-state level, and so much below it.

Jean: Well, it's this idea that we need the creation of new communities, or the reorganization of old ones, so that they are larger than the family, and smaller than the city. And they are back to back; they are neighborhoods. Therein a person would find as much opportunity as one would find in a city, and you would have the human factor brought back in.

VIII
"Trial by Entropy"

Stress economy and environmental depletion. The entropy lesson. Theater as barometer: the remythologizing from within. From technopolites to ecopolites: a new sensibility of ecological systems and global solutions. The X factor: planetary consciousness. The zeitgeist entering into time.

Tuesday morning, January 18, 7:30 A.M. The discussion that follows took place over the breakfast table and a pot of Hazel's special blend of carob and coffee. By this time I had learned to have a tape recorder on hand at all times.

Jean: You were saying before we all came to breakfast, Hazel, that any kind of stress economy inevitably depletes the environment. I was trying to come up with parallels to this in history, and I started to think about what happened to Greece in the fifth century. Greece was once covered with green woods—up until about the fifth century. Now, of course, it's stripped; it's a very arid sort of land. What happened was the Athenian Empire. The Athenians decided that they were going to build ships for everyone to fight off the Persians. So, being great entrepreneurs, they took over the market and in the process began to denude the forests. But they created this extraordinary empire, and after the Athenian Empire they went on to create other empires— Alexandria and so on. And the land was consequently stripped. With the stripping of the environment, and Athens becoming a hegemony, they began to encroach upon everybody else's territory—circa 430 B.C. The Golden Age of Greece resulted in a complete denuding of the Hellenic lands. Athens was the Big Apple, you see, and in order to create this extraordinary hegemony the Athenians had to destroy everything around them. And then, of course, they began to colonize; they had to being exporting the populations.

Hazel: Whenever you see an imperial center you have to look for the entropy somewhere else.

Jean: Yes. Look at Thucydides—the chapter on *Kinesis*—for a wonderful illustration of this, He talks about how everything was turned upside down at this time: What used to be love and honor had become foolishness; what used to be courage had become stupidity. All of the values were altered. After all of the professed ideals, which they could no longer sustain in such a period, everything began to go inward. And so you had the rise of philosophy at this time.

As a long way of illustrating this point, I would like to talk for a few moments about a theory that I have—I like to use adjacent models where possible. I feel that if you ever want to understand what is happening in a society, you would do well to look at the theater. The theater is often an extraordinary barometer.

Hazel: I haven't really thought much about going to theatrical images. For me it's always been very easy to picture what's happening simply because if you really feel grounded in ecological models, you can look at the fall of all the great civilizations and understand very clearly whether it was slash-and-burn agriculture, or whatever. They have always overreached themselves—the entropy elsewhere got too great and they ran out of places to colonize. It's the whole slave/conquest/despoilation process of building a civilization.

I think that we still think that there is a way out of this entropy trap, but in my mind the entropy trap is just a way of teaching a lesson. The entropy trap need not be an ultimate thing, but I think that we're going to have to learn the entropy lesson before we can go on to the next thing.

Jean: Oh certainly. But let me go on to the theatrical images here, because they suggest many things. This is a tripartite analogy illustrating the idea that in losing the environment you also lose your souls; it's not merely the environment that is lost.

Now, in the Golden age of Greece, the kind of theater that was popular was tragedy—Aeschylus, Sophocles—in which there was a more or less internally ordered society that believed that it was sanctioned by cosmic sources— the polity, the civil laws, the moral sanctions. It worked in a very dynamic, but contained sort of way. And those dramas are reinforcement dramas. If a great man rises, and he sins, he goes against the social and cosmic sanctions. Look at Sophocles' *King Oedipus*. There was a plague in Thebes, and Oedipus tried to pursue the plague—"Why? Why?" He finally traced it back to his original sin, and so plucked out his eyes. And then the plague ceased, because man was so embedded in the spheres of the ecology. In one sense these are profound ecological dramas: Man is so embedded in the ecology that if he profoundly sins, the whole social order, and even the cosmic order, come down with him.

So in Aeschylus and Sophocles you had extraordinary reinforcement dramas of the given social, psychological, and cosmic orders. But with the death of Pericles came the end of the Golden Age, and you had the *Kinesis*—the denuding of the land, the rising of empire, and Athens becoming enormously cruel and disordered.

Now, Euripides, who was fifteen years younger than Sophocles, began to mirror in his plays the world of the absurd—the breakdown of value and of the world outside. He wrote extraordinary melodramas; there are no longer stories of the noble being who suffers and is ennobled along with the restoration of cosmic order. He wrote screaming, wild, strange theater of the absurd: *Pericles, The Orestes*—which, by the way, is the finest study of schizophrenia ever done. They are wild, maniacal, broken-backed plays in which the Aristotelian orders are completely broken. And they were wildly popular, which is why more of Euripides' plays were preserved than those of Sophocles and Aeschylus. They were telling it like it was!

But Euripides' world was the world of the absurd. Look at *The Orestes*— it's wonderful! Here you have Orestes about to kill this girl, and Pilotes about to kill somebody else, and Helen is about to be thrown off the roof. It's quite a different ending from the other tragedies. And all of a sudden, here comes Apollo!—on a little hydraulic press, by the way. Deus ex machina! He runs in and says: "Stop it! Stop it! This isn't the way it's supposed to be! Now, Orestes, don't kill that girl, you're going to marry her. Pilotes, don't do that; you're going to marry her. And Helen"—who is the silly dunce of the play—"you're going to be the goddess to sailors!" And everybody howls in the audience—because it tells it the way it is! Euripides tries the keep the original myth, yet it becomes an enormous joke.

Finally, however, everyone becomes tired of Euripides and he is exiled to the north. And in his old age he writes his last play, *The Helen*. At this point he says in effect: "What the hell! The world has gone to wrack and ruin, so I will look at the green world inside. I will find a new order. . . ." So he writes this interesting play called *The Helen*. In this play he takes a variant of the tradition, and says that Helen never got to Troy; it was an eidolon, and idol, that was sent! The real Helen is a sweet, virtuous lady who got sidetracked to Egypt where for twenty years she has been defending her virtue from Pharaoh, who has been trying to get her to marry him. Menelaus ends up shipwrecked on the Egyptian shore. He finds Helen in the green world a thousand leagues beyond men's minds, and he says one of the great sick lines of all drama: "You mean that it was for nothing, for an eidolon, that we fought the Battle of Troy?" And Helen replies: "Yes, dear." So he says: "The hell with it! We'll play the game of the gods; we will remythologize from inside. You and I, old girl, we'll pretend that you intend to marry Pharaoh, but we'll also say that we're going to bury our Greek sailors and need a ship so that we can bury them at sea. We'll take all the Egyptian sailors out to sea, supposedly to bury our sailors, but instead we'll throw them overboard and continue on to Greece and live happily ever after." They had rewritten the script! This is tragicomedy.

Now, Shakespeare did the same thing! Shakespeare writes high drama during the golden, glorious, Periclean age of Elizabeth. Then we know that he had a nervous breakdown about the time of James. James—this doddering, faggoty gentleman who comes down from the north. And, as somebody wrote at the time, "a miasma falls upon the land." England becomes, in short, a world of Machiavellian bloodlust and horror. And Shakespeare, in his last play, says: "What the hell! I will remythologize from within. . . ." And he writes the greatest metaplay, the greatest tragicomedy in history, *The Tempest*. Again, like Euripides in *The Helen*, Shakespeare takes his characters ten leagues beyond men's memory—to the Bermuda. He has Prospero, who had been a duke of Milan, being shipwrecked—again a shipwreck story. And he ends up having to reconstitute from within. From his shamanic, deep, internal, human power he creates a world of Ariels and spirits to do his bidding. He summons a tempest to lure the bad people from Naples, shipwrecks them, and puts them through a drama of the discovery of their own potential and their own law. They become reconstituted, and the world is remythologized from within because it had been wasteland without. And this is Shakespeare's last play—a metaplay, a tragicomedy. Prospero takes responsibility for the gods!

Now, we don't have real tragedy in our time; we have the plays Chekhov, Ibsen, Arthur Miller. We've been through, since World War II, the Theater of the Absurd—Genet, Ionesco, Beckett. *Waiting for Godot,* who never comes. *The Balcony* of Genet. Again, these screaming, wild, strange tales of absurdity. We are about at the next phase now. The Human Potentials movement is a kind of puerile version of what could be happening in the theater: the finding of the basic, core, green world from inside; the remythologizing from within.

In ancient Greece, the remythologizing of Euripides and the playing the game of the gods was taken even further, and you had the creation of philosophy. Who, after all, are Euripides' contemporaries? Aristotle. Socrates. Philosophy then began to be seeded throughout the world through Alexander, whose teacher was Aristotle, and you had the creation of *kosmopolites*—the citizen of the world.

In the post-Jacobean era you had the creation of a new kind of natural philosophy, a new kind of physics, and coming from that the Industrial Revolution—the *technopolites*.

In our time, with the remythologizing, the re-sourcing—the kinds of things that we do—we have the creation of a new kind of *kosmopolites*. This is the kind of thing we've been talking about—the critical density of population leading to planetary man and to global kinds of solutions. And I think that we are about to see the emergence of a new theatrical analogue to this. It will probably occur in terms of what I would call *ecopolites*—a new sensibility of ecological systems in which the within takes the measure of the without.

But anyway, there is a scenario in terms of theatrical forms that may help to illuminate some of the things we've been talking about here.

Hazel: Yes, that's very interesting, Jean.

Barbara: Let me add something to that in terms of the emergence of the new. We are aware of the entropy of the old system and of having to go through the necessary purging. We're seeing at the same time the emergence from that of a new kind of cooperative economic system. We are approaching the next level on the evolutionary spiral. We have not seen that kind of wholly cooperative system since perhaps the Neolithic period, because the moment urbanization became the dominant mode you had structured hierarchies and inequalities.

Hazel: The basic thing was the leaving of the farm. All the cities were built on the oppression of rural populations.

Barbara: The minute you get into the period of urbanization you have these kinds of phenomena. It wasn't just capitalism; it goes back much further than that. But also, cities produced culture, civilization. We cannot judge them as negative. However, we are on a spiral; the next step has to be a movement toward a higher level of the caring, sharing, cooperative the type of economy. So we have to focus on the growth points of that, not as an end, but as the natural beginning of new growth into the solar system—a solar ecology emerging from the Earth ecology.

Hazel: But just a little part of the puzzle that occurs to me here, is that the urban stratification and hierarchy of earlier societies was geo-specific and physical. The stratification that occurred with capitalism and industrialism is an almost metaphysical control. In other words, by the flick of an impulse from the Chase Manhattan Bank to the Bank of America you can order the activities of people in Australia. And that is far more ecologically destructive because it is totally divorced; it becomes nothing but conceptualization— idiot conceptualization. It no longer maps any kind of reality at all. This was predicted by Polanyi in *The Great Transformation*,[4] the idea that a global free-market system was such an incredibly narrow abstraction that it would disorder every local system on the planet, both socially and ecologically. And he wrote this in 1944 when it was hard to see this unless you had spent your life, as he did, looking at the ways other societies ordered their production and exchange. He saw that the idea of ordering a society and all of its resource allocations in terms of making free markets a generalized system was the most bizarre thing that had ever happened in human societies. Until that time human societies had used two other systems: reciprocity and redistribution. He was trying to say that it wasn't so much that human societies had always had a propensity to barter, as Adam Smith talked about, but that markets were local, and not interlinked, so that they served a face-to-face, community function. But the moment you abstracted that, and had this image of a planetary free market, you see the disordering of every other local market on the planet. And you see all of these little third-world countries being pulled around like puppets in this tremendous gale of totally abstract interactions that have to do with the flow of information that we call the abstraction "capital."

Barbara: That's why we're in this critical period. The disorder is increasing as a prelude to the next level of organic order. Teilhard said: "Union differentiates." I believe we are at the threshold of a dual phenomenon—an increase of global interconnectedness through communications, with an increase of decentralized, smaller-scaled communities capable of greater self-management and self-sufficiency. Add to this the possibility of new ecologically regenerative communities in space, practicing total recycling and more-with-less—and you begin to see the outlines of a biopolitics, a solar ecology, a new abundance.

Jean: Well, at this point we have to ask: What is the X factor? The X factor in ancient Greece was the creation of cosmopolitan man and philosophy. It wasn't economics—something else happened.

Barbara: I think that the X factor, besides the breakdown factors that are engendering this, will be the quantum leap in consciousness—cosmic consciousness. And cosmic action. The cosmic factor, I believe, will enter into this equation.

Jean: The cosmic pan-resourcing of the human condition—on global level— is something very new in human society. You always before had the rise of insular philosophies and religions, even if they did in a sense become world religions. We never before had the development of what you might call a kind of collective consciousness.

I mean, just consider the fact that this so-called revolution of rising expectations leads to aboriginal people moving towards expectations not very different from the expectations of civilized folk. Well, civilized folks are moving towards nostalgia for expectations not very different from aborigines!

Hazel: Yes, and that's a beautiful exchange. And we're going to learn a lot from the so-called developing countries. But I agree with you that the X factor is the rise of planetary consciousness.

Jean: And we see this on many levels. You see it in your drop-out executives, Hazel, and I in my common folk—the bakery shop owners, the prisoners . . . This is the zeitgeist entering into time!

Barbara: I find this also with the groups that I talk to. There is definitely the sense that a more caring, sharing, cooperative type of economy is essential. So that is definitely one of the factors.

Jean: Also—something is happening!

Barbara: Yes, certainly. Now, I have a lot fun with the title of my book, *The Hunger of Eve.*[5] When I'm speaking, people never fail to ask me just what this hunger is. And I answer that I wasn't sure when I wrote the book, and I'm still not sure—but that is a hunger for more being, for something that's coming. And I think it must be a hunger for the empathy of the species as a whole, and for becoming a citizen of the world, and then of the universe. It's this universal phase of human development that has been predicted by all of the great religions, and that has been intuited by every great seer and saint. The trial by entropy, if I may express it in that way, is a necessary trial in the process of attaining this level of human capacity. It's an evolutionary driver.

Jean: Trial by entropy is much worse than trial by fire.

Barbara: Yes! It's much more insidious and slow.

Jean: Trial by fire is painful, but this just makes you nauseous.

Barbara: And it's almost impossible to be heroic.

Jean: You can't be heroic in the face of nausea!

Barbara: A catastrophe would be much more exciting! An insidious decay is probably the most difficult, but it is giving us the time to develop this new consciousness, the new cooperative patterns, and the awareness, in my opinion, that we will become not just a global species, but a universal species as well.

IX

Breakdown/Breakthrough

New educational structures: extending perceptual forms. "Economics is a form of brain damage." Infiltrating the media: extending the nervous system. The jungle-drums alternative.

Barbara: One of the questions that I think we should focus on at this point is: What new structures can be put into place, in real time, to encourage and nurture the growth of this new consciousness that is essential to our survival as a species?

Jean: I tend to think that the only real structures are educational ones.

Hazel: Yes, but even that is a challenge. At the very moment when we should be doing this in our schools, Republic Steel actually is telling the children about how great the profit system is. That just blows me away! There you know that the business system really is in a state of shock: It knows that the business confidence index—the index of how many people actually buy those sorts of values—is down to the lowest point in our history. Only sixteen percent of the populations now buy the sorts of values on which the business system is built. They've lost the adults, and the twenty-six billion dollars a year they spend on messing our heads with advertising and public relations—trying to tell us that everything is all right—is no longer sufficient; so now they're trying to mess up the kids. And they're doing it as tax-deductible activity!

Jean: But how many kids are they actually reaching?

Hazel: Well, for example, I was in Cleveland last week, and apparently these packages of films about the glories of the profit system are being pushed into all the Cleveland public school systems. And there are signs all over Cleveland saying, "Profit Is Not a Dirty Word."

Jean: Yes, and we're going to see a lot more of that sort of thing. So what you have to do is fight fire with fire. Now, from my own limited research, I come to certain conclusions. One of the reasons that we continually fall into the same old problems is that we don't have enough hooks and eyes on the pluriverse out there. We have very limited perceptual forms, and those limited perceptual forms give us very limited kinds of solutions. If you extend perceptual form; if you think in images as well as in words; if you are receiving information with your whole body-mind; then reality seems very different, and your conceptualization of problems is very different. You tend to solve problems with many more analogues and variables—as does Margaret Mead, for example. It's just a matter of using more of what you've got.

One of the things that I've been doing is that I go into schools and create programs, and train teachers, and it seeds slowly. And the children are different! Because they are seeing so much more, because they have so much more information, they just don't buy the old programs.

Hazel: Well, I pray you're right.

Jean: No, I know that's true! But, of course, we're still talking about small numbers. So what have I decided to do about it? I have decided that, by God, this PBS is growing up all over; I'm going to create a *Sesame Street* for adults! Nonordinary education! And I'm in the process of doing just that. I'm going to begin filming in South Carolina. Nonordinary education—the use of all these different potentials that we all have but don't use.

Now, I'm just talking here about what one person can begin to do. I've done thousands of one-to-one, or one-to-fifty situations; so now I'm going to use the *agora*—the marketplace—which happens to be television right now. It's fighting fire with fire! Sure, they may have all the money, but I've got a hell of a lot of good ideas—things that work! I'm creating a wild, funny, zany show—which at the same time is showing people how to turn on all kinds of different perspectives and things. And it seeds a trust in the extended sensorium, the extended perspective, the extended sensibility. And from that will arise a very different relationship with respect to the old programs—profit, cost-benefit analysis, or whatever.

Hazel: Well, this is what I build on in the ecological movement. Anyone who is really in the ecological movement—and there are four million ecological organizations in the country at the moment—has an altered consciousness. And you can hook into that reality instantly. I feel that the most important thing that I can tell those people is that, basically, economics is a form of brain damage. It's getting the way of our talking about what's valuable.

Jean: The places of resonance are the altered forums!

Hazel: Yes! And if you tell them that economics is getting in the way of our talking about what's valuable, everyone cheers and stomps because it hooks into every daily reality that they deal with. And that unites workers who are worried about the quality of the work place, environmentalists, people who want special services for the handicapped, minority groups . . . It hooks into every kind of reality. Economics is not tracking what's valuable under new conditions.

Now, I did a "Sunrise Semester" series last summer in an attempt to do the same sort of thing that you're talking about.

Jean: Good! One must broadcast! Broad-cast!

Barbara: That's why I believe that the media is the key; it's our nervous system. If the messages being sent out are wrong, the body can't be functioning properly. Captivating the media and sending out the proper growth signals is essential. But I don't think the problem is profit. Profit—producing more than you put in—is essential to evolution. It's the creation of wealth through knowledge. The challenge is to increase participation in the benefits of productivity—to free people for the next level of creative work.

Jean: And you can use the pathology of the media. The media is only interested in what's going to make people jump up and down, so that's why we need to create the sort of thing that I'm doing.

Hazel: Yes, but I think it's important not to get into the "counting bodies game."

You can get too tangled up in the profit system, the Nielsen ratings—

Jean: Not with, say, a little talk show on WOR. You could do something like that, Hazel, very easily.

Hazel: Yes, but I think that the real networks of the future are really the small mimeographed publications and that sort of thing; they are bypassing television. Thinking people don't believe anything they see on television anymore. All of those images have been too exploited. People distrust television to an enormous degree.

Jean: But not PBS! It has an entirely different sense.

Hazel: But the point is that on the whole people have a feeling of total distrust with respect to television at this point. I don't need a television show. I have other alternatives—the jungle-drums alternative.

Barbara: Hazel is a revolutionary at heart, you see. She doesn't want to be the next Barbara Walters. *[laughter]*

Hazel: No, it isn't that I don't want to be, it's just that the most effective way of giving birth to the new is to stay out of sight. The thing is that the mass hype that comes in over the tube—which is a lying whore—I don't want to be associated with. It's not the way I want to communicate.

Now, E. F. Schumacher's *Small Is Beautiful* got to be a best seller in a very interesting way. This is the new model of how things get to be best sellers, and of how honest communication works. Harper and Row, you see, hadn't put a dime into promoting *Small Is Beautiful*. The *New York Times* and the *Washington Post* had not reviewed it. No one had reviewed it except for one economist who said that it was rubbish, and that Schumacher was a bad economist. So that was supposed to be the end of the book. But some of us, you see, programmed Schumacher when he first came to this country in 1974, and sent him around the counterculture network. All of us did little articles about his book in many of these little publications that really are tracking what's valuable—there are just hundreds and hundreds of these little rags. And what happened after all of our efforts, was that there was an incredible demand for that book. Harper and Row couldn't figure out what was happening; they had to go into two and three press runs. Some of us then went to *The New York Times* and the *Washington Post* and said, "This book is now two years old; it's practically a best seller, and you wouldn't review it. So now you'd better review it." And so two years after the fact *The New York Times* and the *Washington Post*—red-faced—had to review that book.

Now that's the system of communication that I like to use. It's an honest, organic system. And this system embodies your kinds of images, Jean: it's got empathy; it's kinesthetic. It's not just Mussolini haranguing you over the tube. I have just tuned out that system of communication.

Jean: But my model requires a very different use of television. It's a new possibility.

Barbara: It's extending the nervous system.

Hazel: Well, I'm glad that you two sisters are trying to work with that system, but I can't.

Barbara: Hazel, let me give you an image that I use, which has to do with seeing the planet a whole being beginning to come into consciousness of itself as a single organism. The first use of our nervous system is infantile; it's very much like a baby's nervous system. At first it can only pick up a very limited range of signals—pleasure, pain, entertainment . . . There are, however, more mature extensions of the nervous system that are sensitive to the good news—on FM radio, on public television . . . It's an organic, planetary function. What Jean and I are saying, Hazel, is that we need to put input into that extended nervous system, and then we can let the infantile nervous system gradually subside, as I think it will. The major networks are already on a decline. They can't survive—their present form. It's dinosauric.

Hazel: Wonderful! Dinosauric! *[laughter]*

Barbara H.: And the thing is that we have got to be prepared to use those portions of the old system that we can for the development of the new. We can use portions of the breakdown for the breakthrough. The problem with the present system is that it is sensitive only to bad news—to the breakdown.

Hazel: Sensation!

Barbara: And the people in the media become poisoned by communicating only bad news. But if you ask people to be correspondents for the new, for the breakthroughs—very much like I did in *The Center Letter*—then you have healthy rather than sick people as the antennae. Healthy people are attracted to healthy activities.

Jean: Very good!

Hazel: And I think it is a very human impulse to want to turn shit into roses. *[laughter]* So I absolutely agree, and I'm just delighted to know that you two are both trying to be instrumental initiating something like that.

Barbara: In using portions of the breakdown for the breakthrough—infiltrating the existing communication system—people like us can reach more people for less effort very quickly. If it has to be a one-to-one communication—it's too slow.

Hazel: The one-to-one thing doesn't bother me at all, though. Just think of John Platt's step functions—you don't really know which single factor could be the one to cause an alteration in the entire system.

But I do think that this breakdown/breakthrough thing is a very powerful image. That sort of image is the kind of thing that will help to get people beyond the fear that it's going to take too long, and that sort of thing.

Jean: Let me ask a technical question. We have all of these powerfully happy, inspired breakthrough people ready to inherit the breakdown system. Now, how powerful, in terms of their energy and commitment, are all the old thinkers? What is the level of the commitment, passion, and caring?

Hazel: Their level of commitment, passion, and caring can't really be very powerful because it's fairly exclusively oriented towards the saving of their own skins—and getting the money into a Swiss bank.

Barbara: That's the point—there is no vitality. And also, their wives and children are no longer going along with them.

Jean: The breakdown system is turning into an isolation ward!

X

"We're on Top of the Greatest Game There Is!": A Dialogue on Life Extension

Gerontology and psychophysical reeducation: "We are body-minds." Could we reprogram the "clock of death?" The extended-life pattern: life and growth vs. the dystopian scenario: gerontocracy. The technological-fix vs. new forms of community and spirituality. "Throw the mischief-makers a ploy!" The timing factor. The both/and approach. The emergence of the feminine: a holistic sensitivity.

Barbara: Tell me what you think, Jean, about this whole new field that has to do with life extension.

Jean: Well, we're working very intensely in that field, as you know.

Hazel: Oh, please talk about that a bit, Jean. I'd really like to know something about what you're doing in this area.

Jean: Well, first of all, we know that a human being can learn as much at the age of seventy-five as at five. What we used to call "second childhood senility" is actually a shift to older areas of the brain that had not been used since childhood. If it's not used it atrophies and senility sets in. But if you keep the body moving, the joints activated, and initiate new kinds of activity that have to do with deepening, then the person can learn as much at seventy-five as at five!

We have no psychology of the aged in our culture—as does India, for example. One of the reasons for this is that we've never had great numbers of elderly in the Western world. Suddenly we have millions of them, and we don't know how to deal with them. So here is one of our most vital resources—people who have the depth and overview that comes with the brain and body changes—and we relegate them to caretaker programs for vegetable. We destroy them—and we destroy time in ourselves.

I helped create something in California called S.A.G.E.—Senior Actualization and Growth Exploration—which is headed by my friend Gay Luce. She takes groups of elderly people who are ambulatory, mobile, but showing many symptoms; and through biofeedback, through various exercises and various states of consciousness, through touching and being held, through artwork, music, dance, they begin to come back. And they become mischievous, and full of fun, and very sexy, too.

Hazel: Isn't that interesting.

Jean: But the symptoms actually go away; they learn how to relax, and how to sleep.

I've been training gerontologists for the past two years, and we've been creating these programs in various places. With my husband's remarkable work in psychophysical reeducation, using essentially extensions of Alexander Feldenkrais' methods, we can, for example, get an eight-five-year-old woman in the course of thirty minutes to put her foot right on top of her head: a woman who had been very severely limited in her movement. But anybody can do it. It's just a new understand of neurophysiology and the relation of alternate physiological patterns of muscles.

My mother-in-law, age seventy-four, had badly crushed her hand. For a year and a half she could barely move it at all. Her husband died a year ago, and she had to start driving. Well, how could she with a hand like that?

Instead of working with the hand itself, as would a physiotherapist, we talked directly to the brain. And, sure enough, the inhibition was in the brain!

Barbara: How do you talk directly to the brain?

Jean: Not directly, actually. By exercising the alternate muscle groups we inform the brain of the block. You have eight or nine alternate muscle groups to any particular movement. I've seen my husband in three months straighten out people with scoliosis. And many other remarkable things.

As you work with people, giving them access to the ninety-five percent of the body's capacity that is normally unused, then, with the motor cortex being disinhibited, the emotional, psychological and cognitive functions, which are all interrelated, begin to function again. The person will begin to remember, will begin to learn and become curious again, and symptoms disappear.

Barbara: That's marvelous, Jean.

Jean: But this goes along with work in states of consciousness, learning meditation; learning to experience the body-mind. We are body-minds.

Barbara: In Al Rosenfeld's book *Prolongevity*[6] he talks about increasing life expectancy by understanding the so-called "clock of death," which informs the cells to degenerate.

Hazel: Yes, the death hormone.

Barbara: The theory is that it may be possible to repress this death hormone, which has been programmed into us ever since the advent of multi-cellular life.

Jean: Yes, I believe that's true.

Barbara: My feeling is that it's coming to us—this capacity to extend our lives—at the same moment that we are learning to live beyond the planet. In cosmic time a longer life makes sense.

Jean: Well, Barbara, you don't even need cosmic time. In order to understand who, what, and where we are; in order to deal with the plurality of our lives—instead of the monolith of our lives—we would have to live as long do all other animals, which means ten to twelve times the age of puberty—a hundred to a hundred and twenty good years. And of course this does occur in no-stress societies. We need that! Sixty or seventy years is much too short.

Barbara: So we get knocked out by stress even though we have medicine to keep us alive.

Jean: Sure, you can easily stay alive until the age of eighty-five—in a horrible condition.

Hazel: And you're not growing or doing anything.

Jean: What use is it? Also, we're not going to live like the villagers in the Soviet Republic of Azerbaijan; we're not going to live like the people in

Ecuador, with very nice, rich, stress-free tribal networks where nothing strange or exciting ever happens. It's not going to happen. So we have to go the other way and extend our capacity to deal with multivarious realities. We have to learn to control our body-minds so that we can deal much more effectively with stress.

Barbara: But it's normal that we should deal with complexity.

Jean: Yes, but in the societies where relatively large numbers of people are living very long lives they don't have much complexity. We can't go back to that.

Barbara: Oh yes, I see. It calls for the inner work. But actually changing the clock of death . . .

Jean: I think it can happen, and I'll tell you why. Our next book, *Listening to the Body*,[7] deals with this. You can, through biofeedback, speak to your blood pressure, heartbeat, skin temperature, brain waves; the mind has an immense amount of control over physiological functions. You can talk directly to the brain, which is the source of all autonomic function. In biofeedback you learn to control that which had been part of the autonomic system. If you can talk to the heartbeat, and the skin temperature, and the brain waves, you can also talk to the brain directly. This means consciousness enters into full partnership; it's not just cocreating your universe, it's cocreating your mind-brain system.

Barbara: This is intelligence working on intelligence. You get an exponential factor there.

Jean: Yes, you do. And we have seen remarkable changes in people through the use of these kinds of exercises. Through this kind of work you can begin to direct specific things—like the brain and body wisdom improving vision, or developing certain more efficient types of thought, or getting rid of rashes, or possible even reprogramming the death hormone. The body has its wisdom that wisdom does not know. The cell has its wisdom that wisdom doesn't know. You can't tell the brain to stop the body from aging, but you can begin to talk directly to the area that deals with it—the thymus gland—and suggest certain kinds of optimum functioning. It assumes that you are in very good touch with the autonomic system, and there are many ways of doing that: through autogenic training, which is actually far more effective than biofeedback; through certain forms of self-hypnosis—if you can raise your temperature two to three degrees on your wrist—I can show you how to do that—then you can also begin to talk to more complex parts of the autonomic system.

Hazel: In talking about life extension, though, we do have to remember that there are problems associated with this in terms of population and environment.

Barbara: Here's where you have to consider the fact that we're also going to be living in space. You cannot discount the fact that in the next step of evolution we're probably not going to be a one-planet species. We're not certain that you can actually understand the aging process well enough to extend life, and but let's assume that you can. We're not certain, either, that humans will be able to live beyond the planet in space, but we know that we can at least go up and come back. I'm assuming that both of these things are natural and will be possible in the next step of evolution. This may not be appropriate for living on the planet Earth; however, we are not going to be bound to planet Earth.

Hazel: Well, then, that gets into physics and metaphysics. It gets into whether we imagine ourselves as biological beings going into space, or as metaphysical beings going into space.

Barbara: My feeling is that it's going to be a transition. We're going to go up as biological beings—that's what we've already done. We're going to have space platforms, and probably designed human settlements in space in the next twenty-five to fifty years. We will learn how our own DNA works, and as we get the unexpected consciousness effect of being beyond the planet, we really can't predict, Hazel, what will happen to us. But I would assume that we would become more and more spiritual, and less and less biological.

Hazel: Yes, I feel that that sort of transition from the physical to the metaphysical would be part and parcel to leaving the planet. I don't quite know how those two things relate. In my mind, though, that will be the way that it will happen—that we will let go of the biological crystallization more and more.

Jean: You know, people may eventually begin to take death much more seriously. There are many societies where death is taken so seriously that people choose to die. I believe, quite frankly, that as we extend life, which we are going to be doing in the next fifty years, that there will be people who will make conscious choices to live longer—not in rest homes, but to live full, productive lives. And in so doing, you may then choose the extended life pattern: the pattern of life and growth. Whether you stay on this planet, or whether you go up into a space colony, or underneath something, or on the ocean—or wherever it is—it will be a choice of extended growth and happening. Also remember that with all of the mythologies that are rising up in our time—whether true or not true, it doesn't make any difference—about the continuity of life in one form or another, many people may choose to end at sixty-five or seventy to go on to the next stage. I think that the plurality of choice is such that we will not really have the problem we think we're going to have now. It's going to be self-selective.

Hazel: But we have to look at the darker side of it—here is Hazel identifying with the underdog again. If we extend the lives of the fortunate, it will be done by laying a lot of bucks on those few fortunate people.

Jean: How do you mean that?

Hazel: Well, all of this research that's going on right now for life extension is made through a political choice system that is highly prejudicial to the powerless and the poor. The extended lives of a few fortunate people, the beneficiaries of that research will be paid for by the premature death around this planet of millions of children and babies in third-world countries. We must remember when we euphorically talk about extending lives that that's the karma we're taking aboard. That's the way it's going to happen.

Jean: That's where I would have to disagree with you, Hazel. I think it's going to be quite the opposite of that, curiously enough. From having worked in these gerontological programs, I know that there's not going to be any antideath hormone as such. The human system is just too complex. What it takes to extend life is something very different. We find that those who can extend their lives are not the rich at all; it is those who want to dwell in community, unstressing themselves, doing exercises together—it's a very simple form, the form of extended life. It probably isn't a chemical. It has to do with simpler, ecologically much more appropriate kinds of existence that are much more possible in third-world countries than are possible here. That is the irony that is beginning to come out of these gerontological studies.

Hazel: Well, I'm happy about that irony. But we also know that very costly technological prostheses of all kinds can also maintain an unstable form of extended life.

Jean: Oh yes, but how extended is that going to be? There is so much anger, and a sense of innate outrage, on the part of so many people that, if anything, what that is going to do is trigger its paradox, which is euthanasia—in wealthy countries.

Hazel: But there is also the political ecology of superindustrialized countries: resources tend to be channeled towards this technological-fix approach to extending life. The dystopian scenario is that of gerontocracy: only the politically powerful can afford access to this technological, unstable kind of life extension. They will see it in extremely instrumental, impoverished terms, and it will turn into a new form of oppression of life. The more you extend the lives of those kinds of low-consciousness people, who are into maximizing power, and their own trip, the more you deny life forces to the young.

I grew up in a society like this—Britain is that sort of a society. The metaphor that everybody uses in Britain is that you wait for dead men's shoes. There are no jobs until somebody has died and shuffled out of that job. The whole society is set in that sort of concrete. The young have nothing to do but migrate to Australia or something like that.

Barbara: But, you know, Hazel, it's very interesting to look at the timing factor here, in terms of when these new potentials become available. It is necessary, right now, to develop a whole body-economic system for the planet so that we don't have these inequalities. If we don't make that step, the rest of these things aren't going to follow anyway.

Hazel: Yes, it will be too unstable.

Barbara: But we don't have too much time to learn to do that—maybe twenty to twenty-five years. The thing that interests me is a both/and approach—both the nonstress techniques and through an understanding of how DNA works. Cocreation is not just a metaphor. I think it will be a fact.

Jean: Living in community! The thing that happens to extend lives is not injections or special foods. It happens to be a new form of community. And when you look at all of the societies in which many people live very long lives, you find that it has to do with living in particular forms of community. That is the irony: You can spend all the money you want, and do you know what you end up with? You end up with practically nothing: with somebody getting a more interesting form of cancer.

Hazel: The technological-fix approach to life extension won't work.

Jean: That is the science-fiction approach, and people like Toffler and such are all thinking in those terms. But the irony of it is that it does not exist! The whole thing that we're beginning to find out in special gerontological communities around the world is that, in terms of appropriate technology, it is new forms of community, deeper forms of consensual gathering together, and spiritual forms, that will extend the lives of those few who will make that kind of choice. That also demands a resonance factor for a whole new body economics and politics. So the paradox is that the new gerontological approach is creating a different kind of sensibility of how we live on this planet.

Hazel: You can't live longer, then, unless you are plugged into this new consciousness. But people have been living in communities from time immemorial. Only recently has the large city existed—or modern medicine— and the death rate has gone down. So community alone is not the answer; it's only a part—a vital part.

Hazel: Do you think, then, Jean, that what you are talking about will provide the negative feedback to the technological-fix approach?

Jean: Yes!

Hazel: But most of the literature on gerontology has to do with the technological-fix.

Jean: Yes—but it will not work! We're too complex.

Hazel: Well, a lot of things don't work; we're still spending the largest part of our GNP in manufacturing nuclear weapons, and they aren't going to buy us global peace.

Jean: Yes, but not that much money is going into the technological approach to gerontology.

Hazel: No, but I was only trying to make a point. Just because you say it doesn't work doesn't mean to say that people aren't going to continue spending most of the money on that.

Barbara: Jean, are you familiar with Al Rosenfeld's book?

Jean: Yes, I was with Al yesterday. He sends his love.

Barbara: Oh, lovely. Well, he's working on what you would call technological approaches—trying to understand the death hormone and the reason why cells age. Are you assuming that none of that will produce anything?

Jean: I think it will produce very little in terms of the capital energy investment.

Barbara: You think it's too complex for us to understand?

Jean: I think there are too many other factors. It's like looking at the heart; whereas the thing has to do with the whole body-ecology.

Hazel: It's just not holistic enough. It's the old reductionist trip.

Jean: When I get Al in his cups and start talking to him about it, he agrees, too. It's fascinating; I think it's a ploy. I believe that the great ecology of things—whether you call it God or history—often operates this way. Throw people a ploy; throw the minds who can make all the mischief a ploy—"Oh, let's look for the death hormone!" Meanwhile, the real work is happening in other places.

This was brought home to me just recently. I was flying up to Boston, and I sat next to an enormously brilliant young man who was head of a gerontological project. He threw out all these terms, and all these incredibly latinistic forms about processes in aging, and even I did not know what he was talking about! He sounded so brilliant, and so extraordinarily competent, and I knew that he would just floor everybody. And I also new that everything he was talking about would not work. Thank God he was in that field!

My friend Gay Luce, on the other hand, works in communities of elderly people—people loving each other, caring for each other—and she is going out and creating new programs in black communities and in old people's homes—giving people life again. And she does it so simply, and tells it so beautifully. With such simplicity, her mind and soul are a thousand times that brilliant young man! I see very clearly that what she is doing will work, and will begin to yeast a different kind of economic and social fabric; whereas that young man is just where he should be with his heavy words. . . .

Hazel: The bullshit factor!

Jean: That's right. But he said, "Well, I just got two twenty-five from H.E.W. for doing this research." Of course he will! Wonderful. Let him have it—so that the resources don't go to what Gay Luce is doing, or to what I'm doing, or to what some of these other people are doing. Because without that kind of green trash—not capital—we have got to deal with the real, human kinds of goods and services—the stuff that works! A lot of the capital you want to go to the garbage pail.

Hazel: It's rather like the whole Appropriate Technology movement: it must be below the poverty line.

Jean: Absolutely! That's what's going to spread. The other stuff is merely the garbage pail. Wonderful! Let them have it!

Hazel: Unless these things are below the poverty line people will not develop their own spiritual resources.

Jean: It must be people-intensive, not capital-intensive. Let them have the money; then they won't put any mischief into the society.

Hazel: The only thing is that they do put mischief into the society in that they deny resources to those people who don't have survival needs met. So people are condemned to inferior brain capacity, and people are condemned to die because of lack of survival needs.

Jean: I would prefer having these mischief-makers having whatever it is—two hundred million dollars a year—to run into cul-de-sacs, rather than having them loose in a society where they could do real mischief. I regard this as a way of wrapping them up. It's part of the ecology of things.

Hazel: Well, it's funny—I play that game, too, particularly with the fusion budget. There is an enormous budget in ERDA for thermonuclear fusion, and it's all based on rearview mirror technology to do with high heat; lasers, tokamacs . . . But there is never any net energy in it because the pulse of electricity they have to put through that tokamac, or the laser, to get the particles hot enough to start fusing is always about twice as much as you could ever yield to the process.

There is a guy here in Princeton [B. Maglich] who has a conceptual idea of how to do fusion that is very, very elegant. It's to do with thinking harder and knowing what those protons and neutrons will do of their own accord and hooking into that process. This is done without heat and is theoretically an appropriate type of fusion. Well, this guy came around here, and he's got sixty people working with him—but he couldn't meet the payroll. The Arabs are backing him, and the Swiss are backing him. Anyway, he desperately wanted to see Fritz Schmacher when he was here, and wanted him to see this film he's done on his work. Fritz's reaction to this was very much like my own: If Maglich has in fact invented some kind of perpetual motion machine, please don't tell anybody about it! Because of course that will do away with spiritual growth and all of that. *[laughter]*

Barbara: But Hazel, more people will be condemned to die in the next twenty-five years if we do not find new sources of energy. Spiritual growth does not require poverty and hunger. I don't believe that the "small is beautiful" approach *alone* will work. We need genuinely *appropriate* technologies—from people-intensive, low-capital work places to solar energy from space. It's the current emphasis on nuclear power that's wrong, in my opinion.

Hazel: Well, at this stage we're still children in the sandbox.

Barbara: There is another phase, Hazel, that what you're talking about is leading toward. I think, as we've said before, that we're going through a last judgment on earthbound existence. And at the same time we're at the beginning of the next phase, which is the caring, sharing, coordinating consciousness. And this is where the feminine consciousness must begin to operate on a planetary scale. All of the things you're saying have great validity; however, in my intuition, all of that is a preparation for the universal phase and the goal of human evolution, both spiritual and next-level physical. I believe there a next level of the physical just as there is a next level of consciousness.

We'll be able to take some of these steps and move on to the universal scale where we will have the choice, not simply to live to be a hundred, but to become continuous humans and transform our bodies, maybe directly by mind control at that time. It's not a matter of either communal living or medical technology—it's both/and.

Jean: Anybody can do it right now.

Barbara: But very few are trained.

Jean: But little children could be trained in about six months in the schools and could do it for the rest of their lives. That's how far along we are.

You are so vastly overendowed! And as I said before, I think it's to join a larger ecology; to have the control and orchestration to become cocoordinators of evolution, of time, of history, of a much larger universe. And we have the instrumentation; the fact is we have it! We are, all of us, physiological and psychological paraplegics the way we are living.

Living children, by taking conscious thought just as a minimal thing in the education process, can become by the time they are twenty-one years old—well, compared to that we are Neanderthals. The fact is the stuff is there.

This book, *A Course in Miracles*,[8] you're following, Barbara, is essentially an undoing, it really isn't a doing.

Barbara: Yes, I understand that, but there is also a new phase coming. *A Course in Miracles* is the first step in the curriculum—self-forgiveness. Then, I believe, comes self-evolution through life extension, intelligence increase, space migration . . . This includes technological and spiritual growth.

Jean: All of these books of intuition, revelation, and inspiration are essentially forms within a particular cultural context—be it Christ or Krishna—of undoing. It's a great forgetting so that you can begin to remember and use the powerful physical, psychical, psycho-physiological, neurological, ecological investment that is there. You are *Universus* right now! You don't have to talk about evolution. And we've had this stuff at least twenty thousand years and maybe even longer.

Hazel: This, of course, is the only way to get the technological-fix mentality off central stage—to bypass it. I'm not being cruel with respect to these people who are messing around with the sorcerer's apprentice stuff, but you're absolutely right: they have to be sidetracked, almost insulated. And they have to be given toys to play with in the sandbox where they can't hurt what's really going on.

Barbara: Well, why would Schumacher not wish this natural fusion process to work?

Hazel: Well, he feels, as I do, that we are going through what you would call a last judgment, or a trial by entropy. All it will do is put off our entropy lesson.

Barbara: I don't believe punishment and restriction *alone* are the answer. I believe we will be more likely to learn deep cooperation through the transcendent act of opening up an infinite frontier than through living on a planet with dwindling resources and sixty percent of the population underfed. We need to be seeking access to new resources while we are becoming more self-sufficient on Earth.

Hazel: We're just talking, I think, about timing.

Barbara: You're afraid of our learning these things too soon because it will be misused by the old system.

Hazel: Yes, that's it exactly.

Barbara: Well, I think it's very important that we do both concurrently: otherwise we may be unnaturally cut off from our future. It ends up being a dogma of restriction, of punishment.

Hazel: Well really, Barbara, this is the misunderstanding that you and I have had for a lot of years and that we're finally getting to the heart of—that's all to do with timing. What I sense, and I think Schumacher feels this too, is that the political system at the moment is so Neanderthal, and it's so far behind even the individual growth that's going on in this society, that it's too dangerous to give them any more big powerful toys. There's no way with the low consciousness in the political system that they're going to do anything else but take the toys and destroy us. We won't be ready to use the toys until we've worked on ourselves a bit.

Barbara: So what you're really saying is that these things have to be done before we will have the wisdom to use these "toys"—some of which will probably prove useful.

Hazel: Oh, of course they will.

Barbara: Because I am certainly not one to say that all of our advanced technologies we would have been just as well without. If we had not developed any of these technologies—this heating system, for example; this house, this light . . . It's a tremendous enhancement. And some of the new things will be as well.

Hazel: Oh no, no. I'm just talking about appropriateness.

Jean: But the delicate balance of time, history, and invention that we're in right now—we're in the most delicately balanced time in history. And here we have the fact that man's true nature transcends the highest conception of divinity ever conceived. What you have right now is so adequate to what you would call cosmic consciousness, that anything in addition would be . . . obscene! It would just be sheer excess!

We are living in a time of great galloping pluralism, so that one new invention could tip the scales—for not long, five or ten years—and destroy the balance. Whether it's the green revolution, or a cheap solar energy . . . I mean, I'm hoping that solar energy does not really happen for another forty or fifty years. Because if we had cheap energy now, what would happen to man's retrenching, remythologizing from within? What would happen to the inner ecology? Better we stay with fossil fuels and all the attendant problems.

Barbara: You're saying what Hazel has been saying—that it's all a matter of timing. But you wouldn't hope that we never—

Jean: No, no—it's just a matter of timing. If you have schools: if you have places of rehabilitation; if you have places of growth that give man a very different vision, and a very different training for what it means to be a human being—then you would be free to pursue these other things.

What would have happened to the armies of Alexander the Great if they had had bazooka guns and automated vehicles? What would have happened in the fourth and fifth centuries, when they actually had the solid theoretical base for creating eighteenth- and nineteenth-century industry—they had it! But instead they had so many slaves, so many people to do the work, that they didn't have to make the leap to industrialization that was made in the eighteenth century when there were no slaves. You would have had a ship on the moon by the time of Christ—which would have made for a very interesting theology—and you would have had Alexander the Great crossing Europe in some kind of putt-putt machines! Do you know what would have happened? You would have had the hellenization of the world, and you would never have had the yin/yang balance of Eastern and Western polarities. You would have lost your globe! So it's a question, again, of timing.

If you had radical, free, easy energy now, you would not have had any time of psychological, national, ethnic deepening—and thus the individuality and diversity.

Barbara: The interesting thing is that we *don't* have free energy yet. All I'm saying is that we should start now working for it, because we *will* need it. Let's assume for the moment that there is an organic orchestration of these things—we're not working this out in a vacuum. I assume that there is some universal scheme of things.

Jean: We're not the only ones minding the store!

Barbara: I think that the store is being minded by some creative process. We could make mistakes; nonetheless, I'm sure that there are timing factors. You're saying that you hope that these new technological breakthroughs are not achieved too soon; the fact is that they have not yet been achieved. People are trying, and some of them will go into cul-de-sacs, and should; others will probably make it, though probably not next year. The dissatisfaction and stress in our lives is really forcing us into the kinds of situations that you're talking about. Your own success, Jean, makes evident this need.

I am struck by this orchestration of the technologies forcing the emerging software. The discovery in 1944 of the atomic bomb is probably one of the greatest factors in forcing us into new modes of conflict resolution. I think it may obviate the need for resorting to major warfare ever again. I'm not saying that I would say in retrospect that we should have developed the bomb; however, the result of that power has been a tremendous new effort even on the part of the pterodactyls to try to find a new way. The energy crisis is a natural evolutionary driver. It's nudging us toward renewable, non-polluting resources.

If we could bring out the fact of this orchestration, and the timing, and the timing, rather than saying either/or . . .

Jean: It's a symphonic form!

Barbara: If you can make people understand that these crises are necessary for us to make the next step as a whole then you lessen the tension enormously. I know because I've tried this, and I find there's quite resonance there. But if you say, "Never, never, never can you use your mind to understand how DNA works because it's a cul-de-sac too dangerous. . . ." We really don't need that. It's dogmatic and arrogant at this early stage.

Hazel: Oh no, that would be just as totalitarian.

Jean: What are some of the modes of orchestration? It has a musical sense. This is where the feminine consciousness enters in. We, as more conscious biological beings—meaning that we're more aware of our bodies, our clocks, our timing, are perhaps more diaphanous to the rhythms of the universe at this particular point than are most men. This thus gives us a peculiar music and a sense of symphony orchestration. It's like Hesse's *Magister Ludi*—do you remember?—the Glass Bead Game where you really play time and history. We're on top of the greatest game there is! We have a smorgasbord of techniques, of ideologies, of time, of patterning. This is one thing that women can probably do at this time that men can not. It is the greatest game there is!

Barbara: I would like to bring up in this context a point that we've made before—in terms of feminine energy. Because we are no longer maximizing procreation, we are beginning to liberate a new evolutionary energy on this planet at the time when we most need this nurturing, caring, sharing . . . holistic sensitivity. Maternal energy is being freed from reproduction. If it can move into orchestration and coordination and understanding, without reacting in fear and anger . . .

Now, I have talked to the gerontologist Bernard Strebler, who is the first man that Al Rosenfeld talks about in his book. He's called the "Captain Ahab of death" and really is trying to overcome death. I wanted to hear him, and to feel what kind of human being he is. I feel that he is a planetary experiment. He's very far from achieving anything, but he is part of our resources; he is part of our options. If he got too far, too fast, and succeeded tomorrow—but the fact is he's nowhere near it. And I like, as a feminine consciousness, to see that someone is looking into these things.

Hazel: Oh yes, you see he is part of evolutionary selection, and we may need his option.

Barbara: I don't think we dare have the hubris to say, "I am certain that this is right and not that."

Hazel: Which is why, with my friend who's got this new idea for fusion, that I went ahead and pushed him into every loop in Washington that I could. Because he is part of an option. So at the moment he is very useful in terms of intellectuality checking the supremacy of those who are *clearly* doing it wrong, and have all the bucks.

Barbara: The ones with all the bucks are doing it all wrong?

Hazel: That's right!

Jean: Well, you see, what you can do is that you can accept and even seed organizations, not so much for the negative as for the enormous irritation, as you're suggesting. And you can then keep the irritating stimulus, because what looks like this now may be a totally different reality in the quantum leap ten years from now. And you have to trust that . . . along with yourself and the larger ecology that's minding the store.

XI

Women Are Going to Have to Learn to Stay True to Themselves

*The emerging female order: no more dominance-submission
games! Beyond the opposing and imitative phases.
Feminine modes: networking, lateral forms of communication
and a new calculus of self-interest. The psychodynamic correlation:
female patterns of perception and cognition. Female
modes of Right Politics vs. the opportunistic male ego.
The moral authority role: defining the proper questions. Woman
as totally Other. The Joan of Arc role. The priestess role. Original Grace.*

Barbara: I think that each of us senses that our culture is going through a breakdown that is also an emerging breakthrough. That breakthrough has many dimensions, and there is as yet no clearly defined image. It's very exciting because of that. Let's talk a bit about the emerging set of possibilities.

Hazel: Can I start the ball rolling by saying that I think one of the new images that I feel is very pregnant with possibility is the idea that there will be a new paradigm of public order, and that women will be very much a part of it. It's not going to replay all of the dominance-submission games of history, potentially anyway.

Every revolution in history has been a tragic inversion, and the most graphic and tragic inversion in recent history was the revolt of the Hutu against the Watutsi: the oppressors were actually cut off at the knees by the revolting tribe in order to bring them down to their physically smaller size. There never have been any kinds of games, basically, that have not been patriarchal dominance-submission games of one type or another.

The women that I have been dealing with in all kinds of areas, and particularly in the political sphere, have this sense that many of the women who first got into the women's liberation movement were strongly into the mode of "being against." This is of course typical of liberation movements. And immediately it began to move into the imitative phase, just like the black revolution—black corporate executives were wearing Brooks Brothers suits with vests; so women, too, began to parody the male corporate executive and chomp on cigars, knock back scotches, talk about the deals they had made, and so on. But I think we're getting beyond the imitative stage. What I think is exciting is that there is now a new generation of women coming into the movement that are saying No! to all of that.

I think that this new image has to do with nonhierarchical forms of communication based on activating people's self-organizing capabilities. The hologram for me is a very pregnant image, even though when you examine it closely the technology doesn't really fit the image. It's the endeavor to build societies of voluntary restraint based on the fact that people share the same vision of reality—the little blue planet, or whatever. What this allows is a new calculus of self-interest. The old economic calculus of self-interest, when married to American compulsive individuality, led us to believe that we were all separate little atoms. We are now coming to the true understanding of self-interest: that self-interest is coterminus with community interest, with species interest, and with planetary interest.

I think that women in particular are really playing around with these sorts of images. The female style, of course, is the metaphysical division of labor, voluntary autonomy based on a better program of mapping the system in your head, and networking.

Jean: Very good.

Hazel: I think that females are all networkers by instinct. One of the joys of being at the sort of conference where you run into people like Margaret Mead—she's always been a very high-level networker—is that you realize that many of us are networkers—you're a networker, Jean; you're a networker, Barbara; I'm a networker. This is a marvelous lateral form of communication. We're getting away from the "iron filings all attracted to the dictator" mode; instead we're doing the nucleating.

Jean: Breadth rather than vertical models.

Hazel: Yes.

Jean: You know, I've done some rather intensive research on the nature of the female mind, the nature of female psychology, and also brain function. In extraordinary ways my research confirms what you are projecting here.

It began because I was teaching at Marymount College, and I was also teaching at Columbia. I began to notice that if I was teaching, for example, *L'Etre et Le Neant* (*Being and Nothingness*) of Sartre to the boys, I would do it in a very masculine way with didactic analysis: A, B, C, D; subpoint 1, 2, 3, 4 . . . and the boys would eat it up. I would go to Marymount the next afternoon and do the same thing and the girls would say: "Oh go away, go away! Not relevant!" "What do you mean it's not relevant? You used to like the way I teach" "It's not relevant!" "Why?" "We don't know."

It began to dawn on me that perhaps phylogeny was rising. Because for the past four hundred thousand years by the time they were twenty they'd had two husbands killed, three babies, six miscarriages. . . . It was as if they were saying, "Not relevant; there is no context in this education; there is no networking. . . ."

So I said, "It's evolution; it's four hundred thousand years of a different kind of context. Maybe we can do something about it and relate this to your personal lives. Let's start with *Being and Nothingness*. What is it you're objecting to?" They said, "It doesn't relate." So I said: "All right, let's try a different way of teaching. Everybody close your eyes, and in a moment you're going to look at your hand. And it's going to be . . . not a hand, but a thing—an alien entity attached to your wrist." Then I would extend this "thingness" throughout their whole bodies. What I was doing was creating the mind and soul of Jean-Paul Sartre—his psychopathology before matter. All his philosophy is, is an extended psychopathology. Once they had gotten into that they knew it from the inside; they dove into the text and began to come up with brilliant, brilliant insights.

I began to ask: Why is it that good female education has existed for perhaps seventy-five years now, and yet so few women have gone into professional circles? It dawned on me, in observing the way that women learned compared to the way that men learned, that all we were doing was providing second-rate male education based on the paradigms of the male nervous system.

Hazel: That's fantastic!

Jean: Take music for example. You would think that there would be fine women composers; it would be natural form. But there really aren't. But how can they when they are learning the paradigm in terms of Bach, Beethoven, and Brahms?—which is the epiphany of the male nervous system in its best form! We began to look at the female music that's coming along: Joni Mitchell, Joan Baez . . . Example: "Both Sides Now," which is a classic female song. Listen: *[Jean sings a part of Joni Mitchell's "Both Sides Now," emphasizing the circular progression of the melody.]* It's a mandala! It's circular! And look at some of the Baez songs . . .

We then began to look at mathematics, logic, economics . . . We found that if you wanted to teach women, and teach them well, you had to teach them very differently. You had to teach in terms of the networking of information: in terms of gestalts and patterns and constellations of information. Because for four hundred thousand years women have been aware of patternings. It's a contextual mind; it's a networking mind—in the brain I strongly suspect is different! We know it's very different in female rats. This is called hidden information.

If you taught with incarnationalism—that's Sartre's experience, where you literally take on the body-mind—if you presented any piece of information in terms of the music of the time, the smells of the time, the whole kinesthetic sensibility of an abstraction . . . We found that with gestalts women began to learn much more quickly, and much more deeply.

Also we began to change physical education. Instead of "kick the ball" or "hit something with a stick," which are male forms, we began to teach the oriental martial arts, which are actually curiously feminine; they have to do with the pushing that is also the pulling.

We began to make control groups—fairly rigidly controlled studies—of those being taught in terms of gestalt, networking, contextual, analogue kinds of information, and those being taught in the standard way. Those who were in this form of education started getting A's. Not just A's, but A plus—girls who had been straight C students. And it was because so much of them was being involved. It was relevant! If you look at what is peculiarly appropriate to the feminine context, and then you begin to extrapolate in terms of what is the rising female order, you get exactly the same kind of thing you've been projecting, Hazel: You get self-interest coterminus with community; you get a sense of the metaphysical division of labor; you get a radicalization of perceiving analogues and analogies for any particular event; and you get ecological, contextual kinds of thinking. I think this is probably innate in the enzymes, in the biorhythms, in the neurophysiology. I've been giving you the psychodynamic correlation here.

Hazel: Well, you know, I watched women in this country during the '60s getting into the environmental movement, and I saw the way they functioned politically. It was so natural and logical. First of all there was very little ego, and there was a great deal of worry. It was like an environmental housekeeping mode—they'd already cleaned up the living room, and now, my God!: the river was in a mess! They were able to see how that linked.

The way they operated politically was to run interference with the business leaders or bank officials they might be married to and the government. They were running around the community making connections and forcing people to deal with these concerns. I did this myself. I would take some of Nader's Raiders in to talk with the chairman of the board of some corporation and make them listen to what these young people were saying. What I was doing was the soothing. These corporate executives would be very frightened and would say, "Now these young people aren't going to sit in or anything are they?" And I would answer, "Now would I bring you somebody that was going to sit in?" *[laughter]* And of course I had on my disguise as a Junior League lady in those days and looked like one of their wives and so was nonthreatening. *[laughter]* I found that all of these women who were starting environmental groups were doing this kind of networking activity in their own communities. The sense of urgency and selflessness with which they were trying to do politics I just knew was no male model of politics.

What happened to many of these women, and what happened to me was that the male political ego began to colonize these little organizations. And as they began to develop political sex appeal—the one I started with another woman in New York City, for instance, suddenly had twenty-four thousand members—the male political animal began to sniff around; they began to see votes. They would whisper things in our ears, set us against each other, infiltrate the various groups . . . The minority leader of the City Council in New York really rode to power on the back of one of these organizations, and the organization was really taken away from us. We didn't understand all of that.

Jean: Did they really know what they were doing? Did they do it with intention?

Hazel: It would be a bit unfair of me to say, glibly, yes. It was really a lack of self-knowledge. There was a tremendous rationalization, you see: "We can get action for you; you women really don't understand."

Jean: So they were just lost on automatic.

Hazel: Yes. This is the danger of the whole public interest law movement: that is, "We will intercede for you with the powers that be in Washington. If you pass the hat and put money in it to pay us, we will go to represent you before those agencies that you don't really understand." And a lot of people bought this. The whole public interest movement has a seed of a very unfortunate type of middleman in it that I saw all over—there was tremendous exploitation. I see this now with all of the Alternative Technology groups, and Biodynamic Agriculture groups—many of which have been started and developed by women. The male ego—the professional scientist, lawyer, economist, with an intellectual vested interest in some kind of intellectual expertise—will come in and say: "Pass the hat and I'll be your representative because you don't understand that specialized language, and you're going to get cut off at the pass. You need us." There is a great deal of this sort of parasitism going on, which is terribly unfortunate. The men are in trouble; they're losing the old roles and are trying to jump on the caboose of the new train.

So those are some of the things that are going on, and some of things that I've seen where there is a totally different female paradigm of public power and politics that has not yet achieved enough self-awareness to keep itself together and to say, "No, it isn't enough for us to send a male representative to the power center anymore; *we* are going, or else we're going to tiptoe away from that power center and allow it to wither away."

I was wondering whether that experience has any historical background—whether there have been assertions of a female type of consciousness where the cream gets skimmed off the top by opportunistic male egos who've got ego doubts and identity needs. . . .

Jean: Nothing in the ways that you're talking about.

Hazel: But were there any political movements that really were dreamt up by women?

Jean: Yes, St. Theresa and Catherine of Genoa. Theresa actually recast the religious movements in Spain—because they had gotten very decadent.

Hazel: And was the cream skimmed off the top of her, too?

Jean: To some extent after she died, but she held it together as long as she was alive. And it was very good because the monasteries were purified: they were no longer the terrible places of debauchery they had been. In the Catholic church you have a long history of this, men going in and skimming off what the brilliant nuns had created.

Hazel: I think that if we're going to develop this new sort of politics then women are going to have to learn to keep their own strategies.

Jean: Well, what are you going to do about it? How are you going to create a survival school for women in politics? Are you going to write a book? You're one of the few people who has this kind of inside information—knowing what the next step will be and how to avoid it.

Hazel: Well, first of all it's not finished yet—I have to keep testing all the time to see what resonance there is out there. I'm not ready to write a book about it. On the other hand, I know that nothing is ever right because everything is dynamic. All you've ever really done with a book is to have taken a photo-frame at one particular moment in time. You have to make that clear—that this is the way I see it now so don't crucify me ten years from now. That's my first excuse for not writing it down, and the second is that I just like to do it; I don't want to write a book about it. It's all too exciting right now and I can't bear for anything to be happening unless I'm there. If I'm there I can't be sitting here writing a book about it.

Let's go back to this idea of how we help women to see this little danger riding over the hill on its white horse that's coming to save us—but actually is going to screw up our movement. How do we learn not to let that happen?

One role that I'm experimenting with at the moment is the moral authority role. I've found that it's very effective, and very instructive to the males around you. For instance, I'm on the Office of Technology Assessment Advisory Council, and I'm the only non–Nobel Prize winner, and the only nonpresident of a high-tech university. I have used a combination of all kinds of manipulative skills to have those guys practically always off base. After three years I have gotten them to the point where, when something is put on the table to be discussed, they turn right away to me wondering what I'm going to say. For example, if we're doing a study on nuclear proliferation, and we have maybe a million dollars to do it, the first thing I say is, "Well, we must be very careful, if we're going to do an honest study, to make a preamble saying that we're not going to study this because we weren't paid to; we're not going to study this because somebody else is studying it; we're not going to study that because the committee doesn't want us to. But we are being paid to look at this one particular aspect. So in other words, the first thing we have to do to be intellectually honest is to create context: This is the only thing we're looking at, so don't extrapolate from it, and don't get the idea that this is generalized information—it's a little module of knowledge. That's the first moral test of what we're doing, and so then we can go on from there."

I find that you can get yourself into the position where you're always asked what the moral high ground is, and what questions should be paid attention to. For example, I would say: Nuclear power, as you know, gentlemen, is not a technical issue at all; it's a constitutional issue. It concerns our form of government and whether this technology isn't an inherently totalitarian technology. What are the trade-offs in developing a totalitarian technology? It has nothing to do with whether the gauge of one of the pipes should be one point five centimeters to allow a safety margin: it hasn't anything to do with instrumental issues. This gives you a strange sort of authority, you see.

Another example in this nuclear debate: I was invited by ERDA to be on a panel at a conference they had in Chicago on where and how and in what manner should all of the plutonium wastes we're creating be stored. And so I said: "Well, I really can't be involved with that activity because it's immoral. This is still a constitutional democracy and we haven't decided yet to make the decision that will lead to the production of all these wastes. To be discussing the instrumental rationality of this before we've even made a societal decision is immoral. So I would like to go on record as saying that decline to be on the panel because of its immorality. You people take moral responsibility for what you're doing, but I don't want to deal with that myself."

Jean: Very good.

Hazel: Here is one other little story about how you play this game. I was at a conference on the future of the free-enterprise system where about forty leaders of big corporations in the Minneapolis—St. Paul area, together with public officials, had met to interact with me, Michael Harrington, Aileen Hernandez, and Barry Commoner for four days. I had given my paper on the rise of worker participation all over the planet. What it's about is that we're repealing the divine right of capital just as we would repeal the divine right kings—it's just as arbitrary. It's just as right in its place, but it has to be redefined. So I had this kind of exchange afterward: A guy who is the chairman of a very large corporation came up to me and we sat having a drink. He was shaking with anger and said, "You know, I've got a much better idea than you clever social-change people about how we're going to change these big corporations like mine." So I said, "Well, this is a conference, why didn't you share these ideas with us? Tell me what they are." And so he said, "My fellow executives are hypocrites; they know exactly what you're talking about: the question of legitimacy. We have illegitimate power. They understand that, but they're not going to let on. What I think is this: Any corporation that goes above the Fortune 500 level just per se becomes a public corporation. The president, with the advice and consent of the Senate, has to appoint half the directors. There has to be full public disclosure. Ralph Nader is right: they have to be federally chartered. And all of their foreign operations have to be an open book to any country that wants to know what they've done!"

Which is something that I'd been advocating at an ILO meeting in Geneva last year. And so I said, "Why don't you write about this? These are ideas that I totally agree with." And he said, "Well, in my corporation you're not allowed to publish anything like that." I looked him in the eye and said, "Oh dear, so you mean you're one of these industrial peasants—and you're just as much an industrial peasant as all the other people down the line in your corporation, and just as much as the presidents of all these other corporations." And he said, "Yes, but I make much more money than you do." It just came right out of him! And his wife was sitting there across from us and was turning green and purple and just hating it! So I said, "Yes, but I am not maximizing money: I get a lot psychic income from what I do. And I value my freedom. I'm not institutionalized, and to me that's worth an awful lot of money." And he said, "Yes, but you don't understand how *much* money I have!" *[laughter]* "I have got a lot of stock options, and a couple of years my stock options will enable me to tell this company to go to hell when I retire!"

Jean: Oh boy!

Hazel: "And then," he said, "I can publish all of this!" So I said, "Yes, but I can do what damn well please today and I've got twenty years on you. I don't have to wait until I retire." He was just so boxed in! That's one of the things about the chairman of a Fortune 500 company: nobody ever looks him dead in the eye and says, "You're an industrial peasant, and you're an intellectual mercenary, and I don't give a damn about saying that to you!" It just blows them away!

Jean: Women, being authentically disenfranchised for thousands of years, can say all of these things. They can say that the emperor has no clothes and then go about finding him real ones . . . made out of homespun.

Barbara: Because we're already free.

Hazel: Yes. And the other thing that I've discovered about this wild-woman, total-freedom image is that it blows them away, it's so exciting! They begin to feel their chains—and the glorious glimpse into what the world really could be. And there is the fear and recognition that comes with it. It's this whole authority thing of being confronted. So I think that women ought to try to use their public personas in these sorts of modes: infiltrating the existing structures and really confronting the men—

Jean: Wait a minute! Wait a minute! Do you find that they find this in you to be sexually exciting?

Hazel: Yes.

Jean: So that is certainly a part of it. And that has been your history too, Barbara.

Barbara: Oh yes.

Jean: You know what it's like? It's like the old cult of Mary reemerging. In the twelfth and thirteenth centuries people found Mary enormously exciting—because she knew so much and was so totally Other. Then it became the mistress, and they could not touch the mistress. But women started getting an enormous amount of power because she was Other. Extraordinary poems began to arise; Elinor of Aquitaine climbed to power on this. It was an enormously productive and innovative time based on these kinds of things—the wild woman with total freedom who stimulates this erotic need for union with they do not know what—but it is the next stage!

Hazel: Marvelous!

Jean: It just goes right back to what happened in the twelfth century and the rise of Elinor of Aquitaine!

Hazel: You know they're getting right in the gut!

Jean: But it's not biological union—it's union with ideas. But still felt with Eros!

Hazel: Yes! And the amazing thing is that it's a way of them being able to step out of their shells and deal with fear because you're creating a seductive image. It's so much more thrilling.

Barbara: That's really interesting, Hazel, because you and I are in a sense counterparts. My attraction with regard to men is just the opposite of yours in that I say to them, "You have this genius that we—the family of humanity—need, and that you are not applying because you are using it in a limited way." My feeling is that if we could only call that genius into being . . . I'm a Joan of Arc calling the soldiers forth. Their eyes light up—because they do have that genius. There are great gifts among them, but they are being used for a limited, scared, selfish purpose. So I say, "Come, we need you." I convey the message that this genius must be used for the sake of the emancipation of human potential, for globalization, and for universal development. This is such a seductive call! I can see where they might fit into the transformation. So I say to the individual expert, "This is where you fit into the transformation." They might not have seen this at all. By gestalting them, and saying, "Your work is a part of this larger scheme," extend their sense of self to some extent. And I've been operating under the authority of my own attraction to this larger transformation.

Hazel: Now, let me respond to this thing that you do. What I worry about is that it doesn't have revolutionary potential. We can have nothing short of a revolution.

Barbara: I think that revolution is outmoded, Hazel.

Hazel: All right. What I mean is transformation—radical transformation. Because you are mostly appealing to their vanity.

Barbara: No, no. I'm appealing to their creativity.

Jean: She doesn't believe that, Hazel. And because she really believes that she's appealing to their creativity, it probably goes much deeper, thought it might start at vanity.

Hazel: In the well-motivated ones I'm sure that you do appeal to the very best in them. But many of them are pterodactyls, and it so easily feeds their vanity.

Barbara: But each human being has a creativity, and it is being underused in these men, or is not being properly applied. Therefore I take for granted that inside of them there is a misery—because there is an inherent need for creativity to be expressed. When I say that creativity is needed, I'm not appealing to their vanity. I'm appealing to the same thing you are—freeing up that which needs to be expressed in order for them to grow as human beings. By loving it, and needing it, and sanctioning it by my love, it's potentially another aspect of the freedom you inspire in them. But you're not really calling upon the need for their genius in this larger sense. What I'm trying to evoke is the Teilhardian notion of the building of the Earth, the building of the noosphere.

Hazel: Well, another thing about that troubles me, and that is that what is needed now is not females expressing need to males. We have falsely expressed a need to males for as long as recorded history, and the point is that we have to somehow make them understand that we do not have to evoke their better natures by our own need. We have to make them recognize that a new way of being will release all of that potential creativity. They are the ones in need, not us!

Jean: But look! Look at what the two of you are doing! One is coming as the strong, clouting Other, and the other as the loving consort. In the one you're going to create altercation, there's no question about that—and you do that all the time.

Hazel: Yes, but they find it terribly exciting.

Jean: Oh yes, they're stimulated in all sorts of ways. And with you, Barbara, they say more immediately, "Oh yes! If only I could!" But the difference is that Hazel does tend to talk mostly pterodactyls. You don't, Barbara.

Hazel: Yes, I take on the real tough ones.

Barbara: Well, they aren't interested in me at all.

Jean: I don't know how true that is! *[laughter]* But I'm totally different than both of you.

Hazel: Oh now do tell us about your mode of coming on, Jean.

Jean: Well, I come on at a different level that is almost postsexual; that level of male/female isn't even in my mind, so it doesn't occur to them. I come on in terms of . . . priestcraft. The priestess: a very ancient, ancient role that is rising up in our time. It's not a question of any of the things that you're been talking about; rather, it's envisioning . . . a vision of alternatives. So it's taken altogether out of the personal. That's part of my persona—to move into the impersonal. They themselves forget for the time being who and what and where they are, and they become open to a new vision of possibilities. We begin to explore, and work almost like new kinds of anthropologists. And then inevitably they being to ask, "How can I . . .?" And I say, "Well, what would the vision have you do?" Not even in terms of need—need never enters into it. It is the vision of the emerging possible. And then they begin to dialectically play off of the vision. The vision begins to change and to yeast them; they will have been seeded by vision by the time the question of need arises. I am there as midwife and priestess. And you also create, at least in terms of my experience, a charismatic moment of such loadedness that they feel quite removed from the time and space of General Motors—or whatever. It's what you might consider a planetary, or even a meta moment. Human beings have a deep, indigenous . . . let's call it Original Grace.

Hazel: Yes! Original Grace.

Jean: And it is a moment in which I appeal to the god-in-hiding that is being evoked. It's much deeper than mere potential. It's god-in-hiding speaking to god-in-hiding. And then you begin to see the person break out of the individual, local self.

Now, it's true that we do have to deal with the things that each of you has been talking about. But in what I do, a different kind of seeding has happened on a different level.

Barbara: Well, it really is a beautiful trio when you consider all of these things going on simultaneously.

Jean: And the thing is that they all work! But none of us could do the other's role.

XII

Celebrating the Female Sensibility:
"We Are Different!"

*Ritual death, rebirth, and the power of new being.
The model of self-organizing systems. The dangers
of being colonized by male consciousness. Authenticity:
herstory, not history. Beyond catharsis: "It's time for
celebration!" The patterning of the male nervous
system vs. the female sense of network and context.*

*By this point in what had become virtually
nonstop dialogue, we had again gathered in the dining
room for lunch—a wonderful spread of cheese,
homemade bread, and an enormous salad. The
focus here is Barbara's uncertainty in regard to
her own life at that time. This provides an interesting
context for further exploring of authentic female ways.*

Barbara: It's interesting—menopause and puberty. Menopause is a very profound change.

Jean: As profound as puberty.

Barbara: Something new is happening to me. Even though I can sense some older being within myself, and can even converse with it, there is something that I don't have that I need to help me through this.

Jean: What is it?

Barbara: I don't know!

Jean: Give me a sense, a feeling, a melody, a color.

Barbara: It has to do with how to handle the motivation to act.

Jean: Having to act, or wanting to act?

Barbara: Wanting to act.

Jean: Do you really want to act?

Barbara: No, but on the other hand I don't want not to act. Having tried that, I know that I would get exceedingly restless.

Jean: Did you ever consider the possibility that maybe you need a period in which you are acted upon? A quiet asking of questions, reading, talking. And acting in the world, but not making any passionate commitments because you are in a time of change. Why must one always act with passionate commitment?

Hazel: What happened, Barbara, is that you have been collecting a lot of feedback from your past activity. People see you as the Barbara Hubbard who is passionately committed and active. They come up to you and say, "Oh, Barbara, what are you going to be passionately committed to next? We want to follow you!" *[laughter]* And you're thinking: Oh God, must I? I'm not quite ready yet. So what has happened is that you've been encircled by all the feedback you've kicked up. You could get carried along by it. They're playing that sonata, you see. You have to make them see that you're not going to play lead violin for a while. I know how you're feeling because I've been in the very same position.

Jean: You know, there is a very rich tradition for this—for the end of one time and the beginning of another. It's called the Journey to the East. It starts with Ulysses—actually it starts much earlier. It's an ancient Egyptian tale. It's a journey. It may not be a physical journey, but very often it is. The Crusades were a journey to the East, the *Odyssey*, Hesse's metaphysical journeys. Go away. Go to a place where you don't speak the language. Go alone, or with a friend who won't make any demands. It could be an African country; it could be Egypt. And you may find that reality shakes! You come back three months later—or whenever—and it is no longer a question of who, or what, or where. You will have made a journey, and that journey will have been made in you. Things will look very different. You probably have to do this. It can be internal, but with you, because you're so kinesthetic and outward-going, it probably has to be a physical journey.

Hazel: Yes, Barbara, if you stay here people are going to continue to have expectations of you.

Jean: If you were to come back after a three-month break in time, they will not be able to go back to the old image. They will have gone down the time stream as well.

Hazel: And you will have taught them a lesson—that you are not there just to program their energies. This is often a problem if you're an image-maker and an incandescent personality, as you are. We have all been in this position of having to program other people's energies. And there is always a group of people who will expect you to continue programming their energies. The only way to break that kind of symbiosis is to distance yourself and act differently. They won't wait around. They'll probably be upset for a couple of months. But, as Jean says, water will have gone under the bridge by the time you get back and they'll be saying, "Well, you can't rely on Barbara Marx Hubbard because she's gone off to India to gaze at her navel for three months. We can't put our projections off onto her!"

Barbara: And they'll be able to do it all without me—which would be lovely.

Hazel: Yes, of course. I have learned through my own experience with starting public interest groups that anyone who is the parent of an idea must withdraw immediately because the parent must be slain. If you don't get out of it terribly fast, they'll cut you up! They have to destroy you in order to accept that idea as their own identity. And you want them to accept that identity because you want that little public interest group to fly on its own. You want those people to fill it, and it to fill them. And then you can disengage and go on to the next thing. Every time that I've been in that position and haven't gotten out in real time it's been trouble!

What I sense happening to you, Barbara, is based on part of a conversation that was relayed to me that included one of the men who is involved in this project. The thing was that this whole thing revolved around you, and it was going to be a big deal. They were going to organize this thing; they were going to sell this information service to corporations, to radio networks, to television networks. And I thought: Oh my God, they have grabbed Barbara Hubbard and her beautiful image. And who is orchestrating whom? And who is being a sales front for what? What I am afraid of is that the manifestation of your idea may grab you and pull you off into another escapade that you won't like. I sense that the motivation is not your kind of higher motivation; it's ego motivation; it's . . . male consciousness!

Jean: Very simply said!

[laughter]

Hazel: They're going to turn it into a great big profit center. And the whole thing is that you will have made it possible by virtue of your imaging power. But in the end it will be all ownership, control, profit. But, of course, I'm saying all of this terribly tentatively.

Barbara: I think that the distancing is necessary. But I wonder if it would be possible to structure it so that the motivation would be correct?

Jean: What do you mean by correct motivation?

Barbara: Well, the right motivation of those working with me. I think it is basically good. I'm not surrounded by anyone who isn't dedicated and selfless.

Hazel: But men, you see, tend to backslide. They talk about having good motivations; they want to do it for truth, beauty, the evolutionary path, and all the rest of it. But the next morning they backslide and start giving One Hundred Percent Club speeches about profit and competition—it's as if you had dropped an old tape into the tape drive.

Jean: Because the old images are so intense.

Hazel: That's right. They can't erase the old tape!

Jean: It's not even comic—it's tragic. But what erases the old tape? Death. In the past twenty minutes both of you have been coming up with images of death. You, Barbara, quite frankly want to die! I don't mean that in any melodramatic sense, but that's what you want to do. And that's what you're doing.

Barbara: I'm not really sure what you mean.

Jean: Well, we all have to die. We have to die at least once every three or four years. Some of us die once a year. Death—*thanatos*—is a very deep instinct of the human race. We've always had rituals of death, transition, and resurrection. We're the first civilization since the Renaissance that has not had a viable mode of catharsis and death; of dying to ourselves—and then being reborn. Who is to say how much of the neurosis of psyche and history in the twentieth century—all of the catastrophes, the genocides and historical debacle—are due to the fact that we could not die and had to objectify and project it with the genocides of millions?

And you, Barbara, want to die, and your time has come to die. It isn't that you won't remember—you will. But something has got to be let go of. One of the great male problems is that they've forgotten how to die. That's why there is so much killing; that's why they backslide. Probably once a year we need rituals—nice easy blowouts of death—

Hazel: Purge!

Jean: Yes. And you have to go to a place where you can die. When you come back, having died, then all the old tapes in the world cannot play loud enough to drown out the power of your new being. So you leave for a while; so they backslide; so they create this monolith to the GNP. So what?

Barbara: But they're not doing that, by the way.

Hazel: No, of course not, but they do have big visions of grandeur.

Jean: But you will have died and the power of that creates new life. I personally don't think that Jesus himself died on the cross. I think it was probably someone else up there. But they needed that image in order to create the seeding. There is nothing like someone who has dropped out of time and space and then come back again. Everything you're saying points to the fact that you're dying—but you're trying to do it amidst a parade!

[laughter]

Hazel: And they won't let you do it!

Jean: But you're also going to be reborn because that's the nature of the beast. It follows as night the day.

Barbara: Well, I should have died after the Bicentennial!

[laughter]

Jean: Well, I'm sorry, you're dying now. You'd better get out of the parade and do it with dignity in Uganda or—Greece is the great place to die if I may say so. The isles of Greece!

Hazel: The part of you, Barbara, that doesn't want to just slip quietly away from that whole thing is the part of you that feels responsible and on the spot. You may be starting something just because you feel you ought to be starting something. It feels better. Everybody looks to you, because are you not the vision of the starter? They all call you a spark plug, and spark plugs are supposed to start things. When you get back to Washington they'll all rush to you and try to infuse you with this thing that they want you to do. And you feel a responsibility to them. I've found myself in that position so many times. It's also a very "mother" sort of function. But the mother role is to push the chicks out of the nest.

Barbara: I have an instinct about this thing. I think that if I were to just pull out, that it would go on. In a way, I'm in the way. I'm really on another level.

Jean: You're on another level and you're not relevant. It's like a bunch of ions trying to congregate around a zany atom, an atom that has gone its own way. Coherence cannot happen unless you get out.

Hazel: You see that gets back to the model of self-organizing systems. There is a sick form of organization where all the individual ions are polarized around one point, which is the totalitarian leader—Hitler, Mussolini, and so on. Then there are only vertical channels of communication. It's a very unstable form. The form of organization that survives is organic self-organization. It nucleates, and the structure grows out of that without that enormous unstable force field that collapses the moment the leader walks away. You can have total communication in a society, like Indira Gandhi with her satellite, but it's all vertical communication from one leader to all of the little atoms. And that is extremely unstable, and is an extremely impoverished form of communication. The real communication is lateral and nucleating.

Jean: Any hierarchical communication lasts very few years, as we saw with Hitler's Germany. It's like Indira's India—it can't last. Also the place is so enormously disorganized.

Hazel: Whereas you do have that self-organizing, instinctive thing that human beings have—you just let them alone. This is the pathology of this society. The little atoms, or ions, have lost the power of remembering self-organization, and how to relate laterally. Instead, they have this thing about—"I am IBM, and I relate to the president of IBM—*Jawohl, mein Gruppenführer!*" That's the whole model of industrial organization and is the reason why it can't last. That may be some of what you are caught in at the moment, Barbara, as well as what this society as a whole is caught in.

Barbara: Listening to you two has made me realize that I really am not sure at all about what's happening in my life right now.

Hazel: Well, I'm going to say something right off the top of my head, Barbara. I think that my little model of the dangers of being colonized by male consciousness is perhaps something that you should be aware of. I have no way of knowing exactly what this project of yours entails other than the brief description you gave earlier; but I do have this feeling that your baby is going to be taken from you, and that it's really not going to be what you think it's going to be. I've seen that happen so often. You have a capacity to powerfully satisfy the needs of males on many levels—the imaging power and that sort of thing—and they can then feed off of the psychic structuring that you're doing. They can manifest it, and take it over and run with it. I just have the sense that you may be being colonized by male consciousness.

Now, with regard to SYNCON, I had very much a body-wisdom reaction to that. It was to do with the fact that there was too much prosthesis—too much male consciousness. I couldn't relate to it. And I sensed that the woman who used to communicate with me through *The Center Letter*—you had been a very powerful image for me—had been taken over and dragged into the world of hardware and the let's-get-the-job-done mode of consciousness. Somehow I have a great desire to rescue you from that. You are much better than they are, you see.

Jean: I must concur. And that is why I did not participate after the second SYNCON. It was no longer your vision: It was a male vision being manifested in terms of male types of models. But you, with your deeper envisionment, projected it further than it deserved to go.

Barbara: Because I knew what it could be.

Jean: But still, it was grounded in very male models. The only thing that was not male was the circle.

Hazel: And all that gear! I just couldn't deal with it.

Jean: Too much gear! Your image must be authentic to you—not some man's vision that you merely give a lovely feminine touch and charisma to. It's time for your own authenticity.

Hazel: Yes. And you see, Barbara, there is an interplay, and they do feed off of you. I understand that now—you do stroke them tremendously. I know that you are attempting to call up their real evolutionary potential, but in many cases you just stroke their pride and vanity. You give them another empowerment to play their game: "I am the female image; we females need you big, strong, handsome males; I am going to give you another ticket to do your number on us." But you are so much greater than they are! I would love to see Barbara Hubbard as Woman. You could develop all sorts of things that would look completely different, and that would be a much better integration of hardware and software. Your software is superb! But then they hang a lot of clinking bells and whistles and tin cups onto it—and screw it up. And you're left dragging that burden. And then many of us who love you are turned off by it.

Do you know what happened to me? I came a little way with the SYNCON thing, but it was inhuman; I just didn't feel right anywhere in that circle. Now, we've got hardware right here—our tape recorders and all of that—but somehow we are a happy little tribal group. And it's serving us; we weren't put into this machine like servo-mechanisms. Somehow this is all to do with the fact that the males need you much more than you need them.

Barbara: Well, I'm an extremely feminine person. You're right—I understand what you're saying, and it is true. But I'm not sure where to find the strength to go and be what I am. I really feel a weakness in myself. . . .

Jean: It's coming, Barbara. And this need to die that we've been talking about . . . Your death is the death of this dependency!

Barbara: I don't know why I have this dependency. I'm intellectually aware of what you're saying. I know it's true.

Jean: Your story of *The Hunger of Eve* is the story of a woman who stays dependent upon men, and who then leavens their vision with yeast that they don't deserve. That's a terrible thing to say, but since we're all at the point of truthsaying . . .

Hazel: And that's right. They don't deserve it. Your resonance, the note that you strike on your own, is as clear as a bell; it's just beautiful.

Jean: Whenever *you* come through—what a difference!

Hazel: The moment that the males begin to grab it, it becomes something different. They don't do it right.

Barbara: They don't do it the same way, I know that.

Jean: This is what you are dying to right now.

Barbara: What's so painful to me is that I love them.

Hazel: Of course! We all do.

Jean: And why not?

Hazel: We all love our brothers, and they deserve our love. But the new thing is that we have to start gently teaching them about this instrumental, manipulative—the Logos, I suppose, to use Jean's term—and that it's time for the emergence of what *we* have. Her-story, not his-story.

Jean: I think that this is one of the reasons that the woman's movement has gotten stalemated for so long—in catharsis. It's time for celebration! We are different!

Hazel: We *are* different!

Jean: We have a totally new set of variables and options and opportunities to offer the human race. By God, let us glory in and celebrate our difference! Celebration! If you can begin to celebrate yourself—it's something quite beyond ego—in the total authenticity of who and what you are . . . You, Barbara, are equating feminine with the supporting of the male function. By God, it is not that! It is something so much more wonderful! And I'm sure you know what it is. Wait a minute—*do* you know what it is?

Barbara: I hate to keep focusing on myself, Jean—

Hazel: But we love you, and this is very important.

Barbara: Well, first of all, why do I feel this dependency?

Jean: Why do you equate being feminine with dependency?

Barbara: Well, I don't.

Jean: But you just did! You just did exactly that!

Barbara: Well, I think it's the weak side of femininity—to feel dependent. It's been a part of our history.

Jean: But do not equate passivity with weakness. And you are no longer a creature grounded in history; you've broken from that.

Barbara: That's right. But I'll tell you why—it's actually very simple: I don't feel that I know how to manage large systems; I don't feel I know how to handle economics; I don't feel—

Hazel: But those are dying things! They are good at those things.

Jean: Those are the breakdown systems.

Barbara: That's true. But I have looked to men because they were better at doing those sorts of things, and the vision I have requires—

Jean: It requires high technology? But maybe your vision doesn't really require that. Your software is enormously powerful.

Barbara: Well, I think that because I thought that my software required current hardware, I got caught up in those kinds of structures. And the hardware required money, which I had.

Hazel: But that money, Barbara, is a wiggly worm, and it's confusing all your higher-order signals. Wiggly worms sometimes attract not only people who are motivated by the higher psychic structure that you are creating, but also it attracts types who like to be in on a profit opportunity. So that all gets muddled up with your much more transcendent motives; it begins to pollute the product. This is one of the reasons that I would be terrified if I had money: I would be afraid that some of the people being drawn to me were being drawn by my wiggly worm and not just to the power of my ideas. I'm sure, though, that you have learned how to recognize those people who respond to the wiggly worm.

Barbara: I haven't really had that kind of profiteer.

Hazel: No, I don't really mean profiteer. But people have to eat. There are many levels of the wiggly worm thing, you see.

Jean: If you had not had all the money that you had, what would SYNCON have been?

Barbara: Well, it wouldn't have had all the hardware.

Jean: They would have had to put their mind-set into finding different forms of intercommunication.

Hazel: It would have been more selfless because everybody who had been attracted to it would have been attracted to the concept.

Barbara: But they were, Hazel. There was absolutely no material remuneration for the young people who came to work with us; they were there only because of their attraction to the concept.

Jean: But suppose there had been no technology. Those young people would probably have germinated more ideas of the ways in which these kinds of integrations between diverse fields could begin to take place.

Barbara: There may have been an overdose, but I don't think that television cameras per se are bad.

Hazel: Oh no, I don't think that I would say that either.

Jean: But in this culture that much money equals technology; it equals the buying of technological units, because that is what needs to be bought. Money always buys what needs to be bought. You got yourself into technological binds because of that money. That put you into something that grew out of the male psyche and the male nervous system.

Hazel: That is so true.

Jean: Pipes, wires, amplifiers—prosthetic forms! You have the genius for insthesis, not prosthesis. And for that you don't need a cent!

Hazel: You don't need hardware! People will flock around you always because of the power of your imagery. Even if you didn't amplify technologically your imaging, people would be coming to you and taking it away with them to start new communities based on your concepts. You really turned my head around, and we only briefly interacted during the late '60s. You put me on a very different trajectory than I would otherwise have been on. And that didn't require any hardware. It was *The Center Letter*, and meeting with you several times. It really did send me off on a different trajectory. It was a wonderful thing, and I've taken it all kinds of places. And there wasn't a wire, or a television set, or anything like that.

Now, I don't want to say that I'm down on amplification. I do think that we ought to use opportunities to amplify wherever we see them, but when the technology begins to take over . . . It had never occurred to me before that this sort of thing might actually be the patterning of the male nervous system.

Jean: Yes, it is; I'm sure of it. The patterning of the female nervous system, on the other hand, would be insthesis: the use of internal software and the sensibilities of networks and contexts—which has nothing to do with anything made out of metal.

Hazel: Well, I thought I was just a technophobe, but I'm really not that at all. I know that this equipment can be very useful. Here, for instance, we have made a context for this equipment—the tape recorders—so that it's a perfectly organic whole. And it's not in any way overwhelming or intimidating us.

Jean: And that is why it will never die out. But we must bring in the alternate context and the extended sensibilities—the female sense of network and context. Then the equipment can be used as servant, and only as servant.

Barbara: Everything that you're saying I agree with completely. I think I did get swept away into a male mode of operating. But they are attracted to the vision, and that's why I love them. And everyone who has stayed with us has gotten poor, not rich.

Jean: That's really not the issue. The issue is that the vision is being built by them on ladders having to do with equipment and technological structures; whereas the vision you keep talking about has nothing to do with all of that technological stuff! The vision of the new humanity requires a sense of the internal instrumentation.

Hazel: The point is that we have so much undigested and badly used hardware that we haven't yet learned to surround with our consciousness; we haven't learned how to make it obey our purposes. This is what the debate about high technology is about. Let's see what can be done to amplify consciousness with what we've already got!

Barbara: Well, here again, I don't believe it need be either/or—either software or hardware. There has to be a more organic interaction of both.

XIII

On to Supra-Sex! (We Are All Swarming)

The enormous availability of maternal energy to be invested in new tasks. An evolutionary latency? What is the next step after sex? New forms of primary attraction. The cell swarming model: "I want to be in the swarm!" The post-technological Neolithic. A cosmic orgasm? "You are in tantric foreplay with the universe!"

Barbara: Let me put forward this idea of supra-sexual activity—I would really like to explore this with you two. We know that at some point sex was actually invented. One theory is that it was the paramecium: their little tails touched and they exchanged DNA. *[laughter]* Sex is information exchange!

Jean: Whee!

Barbara: Yes—I can just see someone like Disney doing a film on the history of the invention of sex! But anyway, at one time reproduction was accomplished by division, which was a pretty dull way of doing it. But as complexities increased, individuals could not divide, and sex, along with death, entered into the evolutionary process. I have had a feeling about this on several levels. First of all, we are no longer maximizing reproduction for many good reasons, so maternal energy is now available to be invested in new tasks.

Jean: And there is one hell of a lot of that energy around. That is perhaps the most radical fact of our time in history. It's about thirty-five percent more human energy that is now available to be invested in new tasks.

Barbara: Let me tell on a personal level how I have become aware of how this energy operates. When I was pregnant with my first child I did not want to be pregnant. I was only twenty-one years old, and I wanted to travel, to learn, and I was really horrified to find myself pregnant. I felt trapped, and was miserable up until the seventh month, when the milk started coming in. At this point I began to notice that I was having dreams about the birth of this baby, and about loving this little stranger that I was about to give birth to. I began to have fearsome dreams about being given the wrong baby, or somebody would take away my baby, and so I began to really want that baby. I realized that this had to do with a hormonal change; it had nothing to do with my other selfhood. I was being programmed by my hormones to love that which I was going to reproduce. And by the time I was ready to deliver, my total energy was involved in loving that baby. And it was hard to reprogram me because I had a very high motivation for developing myself. Of course, when I saw the baby I was totally in love with it. It was the result of a biochemical reprogramming.

Extending that idea to another level, we must consider that stimuli are coming in at this time from the needs of the species—the condition of the world. Perhaps there is literally a next step of the biochemical programming.

Jean: Surely.

Barbara: It is not by the milk coming into the breast, but by the world evolving. We are getting informational signals that are turning on something that has not yet been turned on.

Jean: It's an evolutionary latency.

Barbara: Yes. And I am feeling that myself.

Jean: I think we all are—a lot of women are.

Barbara: We are being programmed to love beyond the immediate needs of the self in an *intimate* way. I think we've got some as yet unidentified receptor that is getting signals and turning on this larger love—an expanded parenthood. What I am feeling along with that, is that when you get to the fusing of abilities, potentials, and ideas, you get excited—this happens at SYNCONs when people begin to sense the connections. And they want to sustain that feeling: "Can we come together like this again?" I began to realize that that kind of language is sexual. Many people were biologically attracted to one another, but only secondarily. The primary attraction was this creation that was going on. I began to wonder if in the process of evolution the next step after sex was being invented.

Jean: You mean in these new forms of primary attraction?

Barbara: Yes. People used to say to me that my ideas about this were too idealistic. But it is no more idealistic than sex! Nature programmed us to be sexually attracted so that the species would be reproduced; it is not idealistic to have sexual intercourse. And I think we may be talking about a new DNA potential here: we are being programmed for a larger kind of communion . . . deeper than cooperation or charity—a fusing on the transpersonal level. A man and a woman do not "help" each other have a baby; they become aroused, excited, and nature takes over. . . . Being here with you right now gives me this feeling of a high level, primary attraction that is much stronger than sexual attraction! *[laughter]*

Hazel: Yes, I think we are all feeling that.

Barbara: I find that sex interests me less and less, and that supra-sex interests me more and more. And I'm quite sure that this is not a function of my age. I feel a very strong desire to be a part of this supra-sexual activity—anywhere that it might be going on! *[laughter]* We all have to be where the action is.

Hazel: Human beings are swarming in new kinds of ways!

Jean: Swarming, yes. New forms of mating that are not sexual.

Barbara: But it is powerfully sexy in a nongender sort of way. It has nothing to do with lesbianism or homosexuality because it's supra-sexual.

Hazel: It looks like androgynous forms. I think androgyny is the most useful way of mapping it with the old image.

Jean: But it isn't really that; that is still too much the old image.

Hazel: But that may be the only way we have of understanding it at the moment.

Barbara: The fact that women are reproducing less is liberating maternal energy for other functions. Procreative energy is on the loose . . . just as the planet needs it for the survival of the species. When this supra-sexual energy is attracted by a need or a new possibility, in the larger community, it gets turned on and begins to magnetize people to "come together" to do "it"! Perhaps a new sort of hormonal programming is being stimulated.

Jean: Well, what used to be postmenopausal zest is now filtering down to twenty-year-olds. The primary form of mating is changing—it has to! We've overpopulated the planet!

Barbara: In order to survive the conditions we have created on this planet we are going to have this new kind of human swarming. It will be supra-sexy . . . it already *is*!

Jean: There you go, Barbara—there's your next book! *On to Supra-Sex! [great peals of laughter]* And everybody will read that!

Hazel: Yes, you should write that! *On to Supra-Sex! [more laughing]* That's it! But you know I've been sensing this too, that we are all swarming. We were with this group in London, a group called Turning Point. And the love in that drab little hall in London! It was part of this whole feeling of being in the catacombs and all of those images. And they're all writing books about the breakthrough and having a wonderful time together—slopping down hogs in Somerset, and building sheds together, and eating together, and baking bread together. It's all about different kinds of swarming. It's a huge animal energy—everybody is just loving it!

Jean: Your next books! Yours is *On to Supra-Sex!* and yours, Hazel, is *We Are All Swarming!*

[laughter]

Barbara: The energy that is going to be available, first of all by the release from the reproductive task, is coming along just when the planet needs creative action for the future. There is a strange concurrence here.

Hazel: Oh yes.

Barbara: I'd like to add to this something that I have noticed about this phenomenon that I've been calling supra-sex. When this kind of love is being generated, and the swarming is happening, and this deeper kind of social intercourse is going on . . .

Hazel: And having so much fun! The rearview image of what's been going on with young people in recent years is that it's bleak. All of the old power centers see it as bleak and unhealthy. But it's tactile; it's together; we're all hugging each other . . . It's fun!

Jean: We're all back in the cave having a wonderful time!

Hazel: We're having a ball!

Jean: A new Neolithic: a post-technological Neolithic!

Barbara: But there is a very interesting phenomenon that occurs when supra-sex gets high, and when this coming together is happening. You begin to break through into what in the past would have been called agape; a spiritual love, barely articulated, begins to take over. In the process of supra-sex one becomes open to the larger process of which the swarm is but a little part.

Jean: And you begin to reproduce, too. Everyone is impregnated!

Barbara: Yes, women *and* men!

Jean: There's your cosmic fetus.

Barbara: To the extent that there is universal community or communion, I think that the act of coming together in this way makes us receptive to the larger patterning process, and we begin to be informed by it. Psychic capacities latent in all of us are activated. We begin to pick up the God force. Now, I don't really know how to talk about the God force at the moment of supra-sex. . . .

Jean: Well, you have a very interesting analogue here: this whole kundalini notion of stored energy at the base of the spine that rises and primes the brain, and primes evolutionary centers and the thousand-petaled lotus—whether true or not true, it doesn't really matter. But the problem is that it's a masturbatory image, and that's not much fun. It doesn't go anywhere and it doesn't reproduce anything. Whereas, if we're talking about swarming and supra-sex, and this tremendous energizing of all levels, you are then energizing latent evolutionary levels that being to send out signals to the next stuff—be it entities, realities, cosmic consciousness. On to supra-sex!

Barbara: Yes! And that is the evoking of the next level—

Jean: But it must be in community; it must be sexy! It cannot be lonely individuals—the flight of the alone to the alone, which is what is wrong with most mystical religions.

Barbara: Forms of mediation are a good conditioning, but it's not it.

Hazel: The thing that I'm so drawn to is this immersing oneself in the flow of humanity. I want to be in the swarm, and to try to understand what it is.

Barbara: Me too!

Hazel: I remember reading Lewis Thomas' *Lives of a Cell*[9] and realizing the analogue there. When very small single-cell organisms have overspilled their natural ecosystem, they swarm, and then they walk off almost like a slug. They can then go off into a new environment and do another thing. The swarming allows them to unite as if they were one creature. You can photograph all these millions of beings as one creature.

Barbara: If we had a sort of telescope that would allow us to look at the whole planet as an organism, we would see the nucleating that you're talking about creating a receptivity to the next step of the DNA plan for the whole.

Hazel: Probably giving off the equivalent of chemical signals.

Jean: Oh no question. We are a biosphere.

Barbara: Let's assume that there is a cosmic patterning process. We're attracted to each other, but nature's work is even greater than ours. We are therefore receiving the information that we're going to need to achieve the next level.

Jean: This has been going on for perhaps the past ten years.

Barbara: I know that, Jean.

Jean: That's why we're already in the other era.

Barbara: Yes, well the reason I'm articulating this is because I've already experienced it.

Jean: Sure. We were talking earlier about global interdependence and the complexity consciousness—which is a swarming consciousness. It may be swarming badly, though, because it does not know the new levels of order and of Eros/Logos symbiosis. But it's swarming, nonetheless. And that's why evolution, or cosmologies, or whatever, are entering into time and picking up on our antennae and saying: Here is the new information, the new coding, the new mitosis, the new mitochondria—to join with you to create the new baby, whatever it is. We, the females on this planet, are the egg. The sperm is probably coming from elsewhere.

Barbara: Let me make a point here about the way of knowing being manifested here. We are starting with experiential knowledge and then intellectualizing about it—after the fact.

Jean: That's true.

Barbara: All of my ideas have evolved through this process. Now, I have been experiencing this phenomenon of supra-sex for ten years or so. I have found an excitement generated at these moments in myself and others that I literally feel as electricity in my body.

Jean: What do you feel now?

Barbara: Well, I'm beginning to feel it.

Jean: Tell me more about it—physiologically.

Barbara: It is a tremendous animation. It's as if it's a different wavelength. And . . . I *know*: all of my uncertainty is gone.

Jean: How does it compare with regular sex?

Barbara: It's better.

Jean: But in terms of parallel. I'm asking a very serious question here because you may be saying something very significant.

Barbara: For me, this has always been much better than regular sex.

Jean: Is it felt throughout your whole body—like polymorphous perverse as Freud called it? Is it felt as an ecstasy in the cells?

Barbara: Yes.

Jean: Is there a release quality?

Barbara: It seems to me that it's like a kind of prelude to orgasm, but the actual release is yet to come.

Jean: So it's like living in a state of foreplay.

Barbara: Yes.

Hazel: Chronic foreplay! *[laughter]*

Barbara: Oh God, no wonder I need to die! *[laughter continues for some time]* But I think there is a lot to be said for that. I have a kind of precognition of a . . . cosmic orgasm perhaps. It has to do with enough people on this planet coming together in a supra-sexual way. It is this that all of this foreplay of my whole life is longing for. And all of the things I do are in some sense an effort, however small, to get that orgasm to occur. I believe that that orgasm is an act of creation. It's not idealistic or theoretical—I'm longing for it.

Jean: Hold that image, and let's look at another model; I think the sexual model is very important here. Let's consider tantric yoga, tantric Buddhism, in which there is very, very prolonged foreplay—hours and hours—without orgasm—at which point the whole brain becomes saturated with stimulation. They believe that one actually evolves through this. But the whole mind-body becomes saturated with being energized and energized with no release. And then at a certain point the male and female couple begin to lose their boundaries and become one with the God: she becomes Shakti; he becomes the Shiva. So it is not a couple having sex: it is the divine union of universals. At that point the release allows for a new dispensation that floods the body-mind and they are raised to a new quality of being.

Barbara: That's beautiful! So they don't actually have sexual intercourse?

Jean: Well, they do, but it's mostly foreplay. They do not have release; it's not the usual kind of sex. Now, what you have been doing—one does not need physical sex to do these things—is that you have been in tantric foreplay with the universe! And with ideas! Your whole body-mind has been stimulated and stimulated, but you have this hope of release into a level where the personal particular joins the personal universal.

Barbara: That's right. But it's the social level in between that I seem to be attracted toward. I am identifying so deeply with my species as a whole that I am longing for it on a species-wide basis.

Jean: But I'm saying that it's happening on a species-wide basis: everything that happens in the macrocosm happens in the microcosm. We all run into a lot of very turned-on beings. But sometimes they get turned on to—no hope. There's no hope, no purpose, no form of release; there's no real feeling of the new intimacy and communion. There is not enough real swarming! They blow out.

Your problem right now, physiologically, is that you can only stay at that level of excitation for so long before your nervous system blows out. That's why you must either die in release, or find much more intimate, everyday networkings of swarming to be able to sustain that. The biological image here is critical: always try to find biological and agricultural images. What is happening on the personal level is also happening in social forms.

Barbara: Well, this level of frustration cannot be stood much longer.

Jean: You have to die! That doesn't mean the end of the excitement, but you have to find a mode of death and release. Or else there has to be some great connection and reseeding. This is true for both self and society.

Barbara: That's really where the feeling of the network comes in.

Jean: The network is a swarming!

Barbara: What I see in the network—

Jean: You perceive it, but is it happening for you?

Barbara: No, but I can see that that's what would be natural—some form of networking, and something in which I can participate. I would love to be there; it's a joy; it's what I am longing for. And I want to help create it. I want a sufficient level of connection so that the level of awareness is intensified and I don't lose it all the time. I'm exhausted from getting almost there and losing it.

Jean: But your image is wrong. Your image is from what has been normal human sex—you get there and then there's release. But if you have the tantric image, then you can pursue the heightening for much, much longer periods of time.

Barbara: Well, that's what I've been doing.

Jean: And maybe you've finally overloaded your own system, which is what I think has happened.

Barbara: But what is consummation? I'm saying that there is a supra-sexual union with the larger ecology.

Jean: But you're looking for a fact to emerge that will say, "This is it!" and then you will allow the release. The fact may have already happened, but you're not allowing the "yes." It is a release that would be your death. The death and the ecstatic release may be one and the same thing.

Barbara: I don't know, I'll just have to experience it.

Jean: I think you've been saying something very, very important here. What do you think, Hazel?

Hazel: I think so too. I think also that the whole idea, Barbara, of your looking for some specific measure that something has happened, whatever it is—that may be the fallacy.

Jean: The phallusy! Wonderful!

[laughter]

Hazel: But either it may already have happened, or it's—I'm reminded of that cartoon in *The New Yorker* where there is a Renaissance prince lying there asleep, and his servant comes up and shakes him awake saying, "Wake up, sir! It's the Renaissance!" We're also in that kind of a time period: there are thousands of little molecular changes in our bodies, individual changes, social changes—and how will you ever be able to determine a specific moment at which the new time evolved?

Jean: You just have to say, "Well, it's the Renaissance!"

Hazel: And it is!

Barbara: But it's an experiential thing I'm talking about.

Hazel: But the point is that if you are looking for release, or cosmic union, maybe you wouldn't know how to recognize it, and maybe it's already happened, and maybe none of us are given to recognize it when it happens.

Barbara: My instinct is that it hasn't already happened, but that it is coming—I've had tastes of it—and that it is a social, not personal, thing; although it will be experienced on a personal level as well. And all of this swarming is incremental, moving toward a quantum leap. The swarming patterns will stabilize and holistic consciousness/action will become the new norm. The sense of separation will be over . . . thank God . . .

Jean: And by the end of your lifetime it may be fairly well advanced. But your body needs a more immediate release. I can see the strain in your face since I last saw you. You must allow yourself this death! You can't make yourself the paradigm of the whole bloody process.

XIV

"Premonitions of Health"

*The human dimension: feeling and vulnerability;
love and empathy. "Women no longer have to be the
best goddamned male around . . ." The stimulus of
one's own pathology. Trusting the pain. Creative
disagreement and transcendent resolution. The evolutionary
circle: a place of wholing and synthesis. "We are being seeded."
Creating no longer out of pathology or catharsis, but out of celebration.*

Barbara: One of the things that I'm discovering at this stage of my life is the importance of the feeling element: without the feeling element, the intellectual element is meaningless.

Hazel: I feel that very much myself. I cannot really relate to anyone who lacks the human dimension, who lacks warmth. I find that there is no learning or interacting mode in which I can operate effectively that doesn't have to do with loving. To me, the great test of human beingness is vulnerability; the human beings I relate to and deeply admire are the ones who dare to be vulnerable. Anything you transmit has to be transmitted with great love and empathy. If they can't relate to you as a human being, they're not going to buy your message, even if it's right. I think that until very recently, and maybe to some extent even now, women have had to reject these sorts of values, and have had to be the best goddamned male around in order to make it in the male system.

Jean: And that is why many of the great ladies whom came out of the '20s and '30s will not leave a very large heritage. They were unique individuals, but they did not acquire their femaleness.

Barbara: Yes, they had to lose the feminine side in order to achieve what they did.

Jean: But we don't have to do that anymore.

Hazel: No, I don't think we do. But I have had to go through that stage myself in my own development. I had this awful relationship with my father, who was an intellectual bully. But at the same time he was always sharing his business problems with me, rather than with his male associates. It was really a very heavy trip. And so when I was about sixteen or seventeen, I could almost feel myself gathering the pterodactyl skin around me—I was unbelievably oversensitive. I thought that this pterodactyl skin was what you had to grow in order to be able to deal with all of the horrors out there.

It was extremely fortunate that at the age of eighteen I slipped a disc playing tennis. I was flat on my back in a plaster cast for six months. And I was really in a state of hysteria, because until that time my way of expressing my emotional overdrive had been in absolutely slaying everyone on the tennis court. And suddenly, there I was, flat on my back. I went into what I guess you might call a nervous breakdown. But I was very fortunate in having a very loving, caring therapist who helped me to peel away all of that skin. He was the first male in my life who hadn't been laying any kind of a trip on me. He was able to show me that all of that skin really wasn't me at all. And it wasn't!

I was so happy to peel it all off and throw it away.

Jean: How wonderful for you!

Hazel: It was! He introduced me to what was really there. I was so fortunate in being able to get rid of all that before it set me into any pattern. Of course, there is till some residual anger toward my father, but what I now do is channel it into an anger toward authority figures. I love to choose worthy authority figures with whom to play out this ritualistic thing. And I know every well what I'm doing.

Jean: So it could never get out of hand.

Hazel: No, I'm perfectly aware of what I'm doing, and am always in charge.

Jean: That's the beauty of it: The stimulus of one's own pathology creates great works of art. If you can use that stimulus and orchestrate it, then it becomes creative energy. Without pathos, without stigmata, without injury, we have nothing. Christ is nothing without his wounds! Odysseus is nothing without the wound on his thigh! Look at your pathos; therein lies the myth of your becoming.

Barbara: This is so true. I was speaking earlier about being able to trust the vision; I've always been able to trust the pain as well.

Jean: Very good.

Hazel: Now that really is real.

Barbara: Yes, it is real. Whenever I am in pain, I know that that pain is telling me something. It might take months, or even years, to figure it out; but I say to that pain: Why are you doing this to me? I find that where my intellect doesn't help to get to the guts of a problem, the pain will guide me. And then I have a little joy compass: When the intellect comes up with possible solutions, it re-sends scenarios to the pain; if it feels good, then I know it's the right thing.

Jean: How wonderful—to be barometricized.

Barbara: It's a very effective inner system.

Hazel: And it's very homeostatic.

Barbara: Right—trusting the pain, being vulnerable . . .

Hazel: I feel that all of these sorts of values are so essential, especially if you're forced into the position of having to have a public personality.

Barbara: The public persona is the thing you have to watch for.

Hazel: Yes, indeed!

Barbara: You have a public persona, and so do you, Jean.

Jean: Yes, but we've dropped it! And you have to keep dropping it, because if you don't, you get very bored with yourself.

Hazel: And if you get bored with yourself, you can't possibly be learning, can you?

Jean: No. You have to drop it and disarm audiences. You know—"Don't believe much of anything I say!" *[laughter]* And if you're doing tricks, you should inform the audience: "Look at what I've just done to you!"

Hazel: Barbara and I want to do exactly this kind of thing with the debate on technology that we're doing before Congress. We want to be transparent before them, and to show them that this is definitely no male number. First of all, there is the complementarity principle: We refuse to be thrown in there like a couple of female wrestlers.

Jean: Creative disagreement!

Hazel: Yes, exactly. And also, we want to show them that not only are we able to examine our own motives without getting uptight, but also that we are able to show *them* our motives. And that's a very dangerous thing to do in a place like Washington! You can imagine what the reaction to this sort of thing would be to a Washington type person: "Well, have those two women ever put the lid on their public ambitions: we've got the dirt on them now! They've exposed all of their psychological hangups and all of that, and so they have disqualified themselves from ever running for public office!" But I want to expose myself; I want to be vulnerable! I don't want to be part of a system that judges people in that inhumane a way. It will be a great learning experience for them if you and I can do that, Barbara.

Jean: Wonderful! When does this debate take place?

Hazel: On the eighth of June. There will be all of the technophiles on one side and all of the technophobes on the other.

Barbara: Two teams! One rooting for me, and the other for Hazel! *[laughter]*

Hazel: But we're just not going to play that game.

Barbara: What's been happening, Hazel, in probing each other's motivations, is that a new kind of thing is emerging between us. I don't believe that we really are in disagreement, even though our respective teams would think that we are. My conception, for instance, of the development of space technology, you would not object to. You are objecting to it if it's done in the old manipulative, destructive way.

Hazel: That's right. If the males are colonizing the vision, then it's no good.

Barbara: Yes. What I mean by the physical extension of humanity into space could not be done in the old way. I don't want that either.

Hazel: No, I know you don't.

Barbara: I wouldn't like it, though, if you were to say that under no circumstances would you want this to happen. But when you say that you don't want it to happen in terms of the old consciousness, I have to agree with you.

Hazel: And it's going to be so interesting to see how they deal with the fact that you and I share a body of beliefs, and that we're each playing out an aspect of it in terms of the way that we feel best constituted to do it.

Barbara: And it's been a healing act; it's been healing for me to realize that there is a transcendent resolution of this difference. It also might be healing to others if we can thus expose ourselves.

Hazel: That's right. We should expose ourselves; we should be vulnerable.

The thing is that we do share a body of beliefs, and both of our roles are essential. Barbara is acting out the part of the human race that says, "I want to go! Let's go and explore!" In Jungian terms, this might be an expression of the Pathfinder archetype. I'm saying, on the other hand, "Now, are you sure you've got your lunch packed? Are you sure that you have a good map?" This is merely the expression of a different, but complementary, archetype. These roles are all necessary; they just have to be orchestrated.

Barbara: I feel the need for your role in terms of my own expectations: I know that I wouldn't worry about the lunch box. And I would be infiltrated by colonists because I'm overreceptive.

Jean: Will you continue to be this receptive to that after these conversations? These conversations are change agents; we are being seeded. As a result of these conversations that we've had in the last twenty hours or so, do you feel in any way different? How have they changed you?

Barbara: Well, first of all, I feel premonitions of health. I had been having a hard time dealing with how to act because I was so low in energy. I needed some modicum of health in order to have the strength to do what I have to do.

Jean: Will you be going back into that capitulating role?

Barbara: No. I would be premature if I said that I know exactly what I'm going to do, but I do know that I will no longer be responsible for that which I don't really want to be responsible for.

Hazel: And this whole business of relating to male consciousness when you have such a beautiful female consciousness—this is what I want you to focus on. How are you going to express your contribution to feminine consciousness—to the new story; which is *her*story, not *his*tory?

Barbara: Well, there were several signals that came to me in meditation before coming here: one was "travel," the second was "evolutionary circle," and also "teaching"—though not in terms of standing in front of a class. There was also the idea of a voice—the radio. So those are elements in what I'm going to do. First of all, I'm going to travel in order to get away from everything, and also in order to experience this death that we've been talking about. I want to take along my tape recorder, and spend a lot of time just talking with people, particularly with a number of young women I know who are very much interested in this new consciousness. I may even team up with them in some way. Perhaps in creating replicas of this little group, and taping those conversations, a radio thing may emerge.

Of all the people I know, I really consider you two to be the mostly deeply related to this. This is to me a real core of something I have never had in my life with other women. I have always had a deep feeling for both of you, but unfortunately we've never really taken the time to pursue these deeper levels before.

Jean: Yes, how unfortunate!

Barbara: I would say that you two are very deeply related to the things that are happening in the world, and to what is happening to me. This circle might be for me a touchstone; I need place to come back to.

Hazel: And it's cozy.

Barbara: Yes, I need a cozy place to come back to that isn't depending on me for anything except our mutual growth.

Jean: It's a place of wholing. Not even healing—it's wholing. But, you know, healing, health, whole and agricultural balance all come from the same root word: *hal* in Old English.

Barbara: Wholing, yes.

Jean: And it's a nice supra-sexy swarming! *[laughter]*

Hazel: And it's a place of synthesis.

Barbara: This is an evolutionary circle. This time it has mostly been a place of synthesis for me, but on future occasions—

Jean: Its rhythms will vary according to who is at the place of pain. The focus will vary. Hazel and I were not a places of pain this time.

Hazel: But I've been relating very strongly to Barbara because I'm very close to running into some of the pitfalls that she's been running into.

Jean: So she has in a sense been a model for you, and has helped you to work some things out for yourself.

Hazel: Oh yes. Every time I'm wagging my finger at Barbara, and telling her what to do, I'm really telling myself at the same time. I've been thinking about this for several months; that I don't like what could be happening to me; that it's time for me to do a new thing. That was so beautiful for me when you talked about the death thing. I have been feeling that same thing, almost shamefully: How nice it would be to die!

Jean: But it's a deep need.

Hazel: So this whole thing has been a lovely experience for me. Your feelings, Barbara, were really a gift to me because they enabled me to catharsize.

Barbara: And perhaps not have to go this far into whatever it is.

Hazel: Exactly.

Barbara: One of the things that I feel we should stress as part of the feminine role in the transformation, is that we want to do it as best as humanly possible without destroying. Almost every major transition in history has resulted in so much destruction and pain that that pain was carried over into the new era. We want to do it without pain.

Hazel: To do it right.

Barbara: To do it without violence psychologically, as well as physically. What we've been groping for is a way that frees the other to be something better as well.

Hazel: I still reserve the right to say that some people need to be psychologically roughed up a little.

Barbara: I don't deny that. But once, Hazel, you're in the position of empowering the transition, then you'd better be sure you're not doing it with hurt built in.

Hazel: With my hurt built in.

Jean: And also remember that there's a difference between roughing up and hurt that will then bear the fruit of hurt. It's the difference between creation and catharsis.

Hazel: Yes, I must be very careful about that.

Jean: Make sure it's done as creation, not catharsis. Creation has birth pangs, but it doesn't have utter voiding.

Barbara: It can't be vengeful.

Jean: No, there can be no vengeance.

Barbara: You see, if you hurt out of catharsis, but not vengeance, it's okay But if you feel any vengeance, then it's going to have repercussions on many levels.

Hazel: That is definitely something that I have to watch out for in myself: thinking that I've made the catharsis of all my hurt, and then finding, as I've just done in the last few minutes, that it's still there.

Jean: Hazel, do you ever actively forgive your father?

Hazel: Yes. I've tried to on the conscious level, but then I realize that I never really have.

Jean: Well, it's a very useful exercise to go back in your mind and find yourself as a little girl. You talk with that little girl, and help her to understand, and to forgive your father.

Hazel: Well, I did begin to understand when I was about ten. I knew then that his mother had never hugged him, had never loved him, and sent him away at the age of eight. I knew very much why he was the way he was. I had intellectually forgiven him; but still, when I had to deal with him, I put four thousand miles between myself and him.

Jean: When you were how old?

Hazel: Twenty-one. The first time I saw him again, maybe five years later, I thought that I'd finally gotten rid of all that anger. And yet, the moment he walked into the room, I bristled. And I realized that all of that intellectualizing hadn't really done anything.

Jean: Well, it's almost done with a sense of poignancy, and pain, and tears. It's a release in the heart. It's almost as if you're forgiving his eight-year-old self.

Hazel: Yes, I wish I could do that.

Jean: Is he still alive?

Hazel: No. That's why I feel very badly about it. When somebody dies, then for God's sake, you ought to be able to forgive him.

Jean: Do you accept continuity of life in some form or another?

Hazel: Yes, I suppose.

Jean: There is a way in which you actually enter into the universe, and you find that being who continues in some way or form, and you forgive him. One can forgive at any level. But it is only in the moment of forgiveness that you have the true catharsis of that kind of emotion; otherwise it will plague you for the rest of your life.

Hazel: Yes, I really have to do that. What I've been doing until now is using that anger, and channeling it.

Jean: But suppose you didn't have to do that anymore. You've done that. Suppose you were able to create no longer out of pathology, but out of celebration.

Hazel: Yes. And that is why I'm going through a change, too. I've done that, and I've tried to do it wisely; I've tried to choose worthy figures for this catharsis. *[laughter]* But I'm pretty bored with that pattern now. So this is what I'm going to try to deal with as a result of these conversations.

XV

"We Must *Be* the Way!"

*Revolutionary zeal. The court jester role: "The emperor
has no clothes!" The seductive image of the other side:
enacting the vision. A change of sensibility: a higher,
queenly comedy. "The divine right of queens!" Planetary
hostelry and the seeding of ideas. Love as the transforming agent.
"Women must recognize themselves as primary channels of godfulness."*

Hazel: Although I do want to get rid of some of the anger out of which I've been operating, there is a part of me that wants to be more revolutionary. One part of me is fighting that, and the other part of me is saying, "Who else will be a revolutionary and fight all these terrible injustices if I don't? Not enough people really care about the pain. Who will bring these criminals to justice if not me?" *[laughter]*

Jean: "And who will redress my pain?"

Hazel: My pain, yes . . .

Jean: "Who will redress what my father did to me?"

Hazel: Yes . . . I know that the pain out there is something that I can relate to because I have felt it, too. I identify very strongly with people that are being oppressed. It's not only Hazel being put upon as a child, but really identifying with empty rice bowls, and with all of the people in this society who are systematically screwed. I just get so upset about it, and think that if I don't cultivate my revolutionary zeal—let's go back to nineteenth-century Marxist images for a moment—who else will? This is my problem: I do believe that somebody has got to do this role. If I decide to cop out of that role, there are very few people who will do it. Very few people have the courage; it requires courage to do that. And I have set myself up to do this role—the court jester who can announce that the emperor has no clothes.

Jean: But what would be the role that would grow organically from this for a moment, and look at it as a model. What would grow organically from the court jester?

Hazel: Well, obviously a more visionary role in terms of the new. Part of me has been trying desperately to do that.

Jean: Is it a small part, or a very loaded part? Where does the passion lie? Passion always moves around one's body-mind; where is it moving to?

Hazel: From the jester role?

Jean: Is the passion still in the jester, or are you being impassioned and empowered as a visionary?

Hazel: No, I'm still very much centered in the jester role. I know how powerful and important the visionary role is, and the mapping of the new system . . .

Jean: In a sense you're already trying to do that. Your recent papers are all transition role papers.

Hazel: Yes, they are. Very much so. They're all transition-role oriented. The thing I'm afraid of, though, is that if you keep writing and talking about the transition without dealing with people who already have power, and who don't want it to happen, then you might as well join all the other "veggies." California is just full of them.

Jean: Yes, it's terrible.

Barbara: But that's not the only alternative.

Jean: No, it isn't. Now, you're an active muscular being, Hazel; you're a strong, healthy lady. This kind of muscular sensibility means that you have to enact the vision; you can't just write about it. The power of a vision seen so vitally that one is living it out is so much more powerful than a vision of transition. My feeling in reading some of your papers, is that you are exploring, and doing a lot of transition bridgework, but that you do not yet live on the other side. It's like Moses, who got stuck on the rock and never moved on to Canaan.

Hazel: I don't live on the other side.

Jean: No, you don't.

Hazel: But relate very strongly to those who do. I think that, for me, moving to a farm in the South, which I hope to do eventually, will be a way of getting to the other side.

Jean: But there are other ways of living on the other side that would enable you to appear as a powerful incarnation of the other side, and not just as someone who points out the way. Then one becomes so much more powerful—because one is sanctioned and mandated from the next stage!

Hazel: Well, you see, the powerful part of the jester role is the part that suggests the seductive image of the wild woman that I was talking about earlier. I am trying to embody something that is beyond all those crumbling structures. That's the part of the jester role that is evolutionary. There is the power of the beckoning—but in a very naughty, teasing way.

Jean: Well, you are a comedian.

Hazel: Yes.

Jean: But it's always Pagliacci—"laugh, clown, laugh"—and he never really gets there himself. That's the story of Pagliacci.

I remember an LSD subject of mine; LSD subjects tend to make wonderful puns. This particular subject was having a tremendous revelation about Cartesian duality, and he shouted out this rather funny poem, if I can remember it: "I see behind the duality blind/And before this state I rise in kind/To king's own jester, fool sublime/Immortal idiot, godly mine." And it was a wonderful place. That was the place of John the Baptist, by the way. Now, only you can answer this question: Are you John, or can you be Jesus? John is the one who points the way; Jesus the one who becomes the way. Jesus had the chutzpah to embody the image, and to say, "Here I am; I am the Way!"

Hazel: I'm not sure I fully understand that metaphor.

Jean: Well, you are talking about a state of rising frustration because of a change occurring yourself. You've done a certain things—brilliantly—for years now, as Barbara has, and you know that, like Barbara, you are in danger of falling into certain traps. Now, I'm in a somewhat different state; I've just come out of that kind of thing only recently, thus I may wax rhetorical. You're talking about a level of frustration with the critical density of what you have done; clownishness can get you so far, and then you know that you've gotten stuck in this feedback with yourself. It gets to be cloying, and you don't quite like your own reality.

Hazel: Right.

Jean: Some other beingness is about to rise in you, and yet you are still doing the same kinds of things. The beingness that I sense rising in you is beyond the one who points out the way, and is becoming the one who can embody the image and say: I *am* the way. In this sense you take on the full resonance of the reality that is to come. Do you see what I mean? Do you follow this metaphor?

Hazel: Yes, I think I do. In some ways it's frightening.

Jean: Oh, it's horrible!

Hazel: Well, it sounds rather like one would be setting oneself up for crucifixion.

Jean: No, no! To hold your sensibility up in a state of joy and celebration—

Barbara: May I say something here about crucifixions? If we are right about this transition being inherent, and moving toward greater good—crucifixions come when you're premature. If you're right, but premature, that's deadly.

Jean: Then you get into radical martyrdom.

Barbara: Let's assume we're not premature.

Jean: And let's assume you're saying: I *am*, because we *are*. That's something different; it's not an insular base, as was the case with Jesus, for instance.

Hazel: I have often thought to myself: How strong am I? And how much am I willing to expose myself to? The people I admire are the ones who take tremendous risks: They get the FBI on them; their phones are tapped . . .

Jean: But you aren't taking those sorts of risks.

Hazel: I could. You see, that's one route of going forward.

Jean: That's one, but there are other routes.

Barbara: That's the old form of revolutionary, Hazel.

Jean: That's Daniel Ellsberg—a professional martyr.

Hazel: The thing is that I'm not that at all.

Jean: No. We're talking about a new state of being; a state of joy and celebration. The FBI wouldn't know what to do with joy and celebration! If you're giving out signals that they don't know how to deal with, it does not compute. They'll go worry about somebody else whose signals do compute.

Hazel: But I really don't know how to throw out those signals. There are many people who are doing the new thing: some of them are doing it with biodynamic agriculture; some of them are doing it like John and Nancy Todd at the New Alchemy Institute; some of them are doing it like Bill Thompson at Lindisfarne . . . I've been assessing my capabilities for about a year now, and

I like the image of planetary hostelry, which is almost Madame de Stael image in some respects. And yet, I also very much want to go around dropping seeds in the form of ideas. I call myself a Johnny Appleseed of cheap ideas.

Jean: But they're not cheap ideas; they may be critical.

Hazel: What I mean when I talk about cheap ideas, is that ideas are very much easier than implementation. I couldn't implement my way out of a paper bag!

Jean: But seeding ideas is already a form of implementation. If we just throw the seed in the ground, and trust nature, the tree will take root and come up by itself.

Hazel: Yes, I've learned a great deal about that. I've seeded a lot of organizations in the past ten years. To the extent to which I was able to find the right person, I could then back off and let the organization grow by itself.

Jean: Right. But don't you see that you need not necessarily change your pattern of activity? You can continue doing what comes naturally, and the organic extensions of that: but you must allow a change of sensibility. It must become a higher comedy! Not low comedy, as in the jester—but a higher, queenly comedy.

Hazel: But first I have to work on purging the last vestiges of hurt.

Jean: Right. But a change in sensibility would already give you so much more—power is not the word, but *potentia*. It's that seeding charisma. You don't have to fight people; you just appear; you *are*; and they are seeded. The divine right of queens! *[laughter]*

Hazel: Yes. You see, at one time I was afraid to let go of the anger, because I thought that it was the steam engine that was driving me.

Jean: Well, it probably was for a while.

Hazel: It was. And if I had purged the anger five years ago, I probably wouldn't have done half of what I've done.

Jean: No, you needed the anger then. But you no longer do.

Hazel: No, you're so right. I used to be my security blanket. I know now, though, that when I get up in the morning I will be just full of piss and vinegar, but it's no longer to do with anger. I used to think that it was only because I had this head of steam on. But I'm realizing more and more that I just don't need that anymore. And thank you both for reinforcing that.

Barbara: You know, I think what is behind all this, is the idea of love as the transforming agent. What we're saying, Hazel, is that you have to begin to operate no longer out of anger, but out of love—doing very much the same kind of thing you're been doing.

Hazel: Yes, that's right, because I'm really not unhappy with the way it's all playing out logistically.

Barbara: With all of the intelligence that you bring to bear on it, you won't need that anger at all if you can operate out of love.

Hazel: No, it is becoming unbecoming, isn't it? *[laughter]*

Jean: You're past the stage in your life where it was appropriate.

Barbara: Jean, one of the things that prompted me to call us together in this was, was when you asked me who I identified with—Christ or Paul. I answered, "Oh, St. Paul. If I identify with anybody it's certainly not Christ!" And you said, "Why not?!" *[laughter]* By God, it's time that women recognized themselves as primary channels of godfulness! Why not? Why should we forever identify ourselves as the one who carries it out, rather than as the one who *is* it.

Hazel: Yes! We *are* it!

Barbara: We are! This is part of the emergence of the feminine in our time: We must become the way! We must *be* the way!

be the way!

POSTSCRIPT

April 27, 1978; Princeton, New Jersey. More than a year since the four of us were last together. Looking back, now, at the transcriptions of that first meeting makes us all aware of time and flux. There is an urge to alter ideas, to fit them more neatly into the present kaleidoscopic time frame. But ideas, as everything, are time-specific; this manuscript captures a brief moment in a continuous, dramatic process. And so we move on: New ideas, new themes, new points of growth.

Listening to the conversations now taking place over second cups of coffee, it occurs to me that a new book would be required to adequately record this new convergence. Here is the raw material—a new book, perhaps, on the subject that keeps urging itself into this morning's brainstorming; that is, the new political forms that must arise in response to the emerging new consciousness. But for the moment this is not my intent.

There is something that happens when the three of you come together that I see as being the central message of this manuscript . . .

— Yes! Our message is that although we are three very different people, and although we manifest ourselves in three very different ways, we have a process together that we trust.

— And that creates the new hope! Between us we create one very decent human being. Now that's something very new. Before it had always been teamwork!: people who keep their individuality and somehow don't get lost in the process of making connections. But what happens here is what I mean when I talk about leaky margins.

— What we are saying is that the process we create when we're together turns out to be something that we all respect and treasure.

— Synergy! The whole is greater than the sum of the parts! We create something very different than, and in a way unpredictable from, the individual parts.

— And we know it's unpredictable, but we are willing to trust the process.

— What happens is always unique, and is uniquely precious every time.

— Yes, because of the beautiful orchestration of evolving human souls. Look at the amount of growth we have all experienced since our first meeting. And that really is part of the power of this interaction—that you're enlarging your own center to encompass all the permutations and combinations of ideas and energies.

Yes, this is precisely what it's all about. There is a process going on in this interaction that is no mere footnote to all the intellectual positioning I have duly transcribed. This is a communion: a self-creating nexus from which issues a common alignment of roles and visions. And it's *supra-sexy.* Supercharged and *swarming!*—not unlike a chemical reaction in which all the elements are transformed. . . .

Hazel: I've been thinking a lot about what I learned from that first interaction a year ago. First of all, I feel like the most pragmatic of the three of us. I'm trying to prepare people's heads for what has to come. This is the role that I feel I have to play. I learned from Jean that I could be a better transformer if I allowed more of my repressed spiritual needs to come through. So what I've been doing the past year is learning how to get these very pragmatic types I deal with to experience the very real spiritual thing that I experience. I now dare to say spiritual things in places where it's not expected. I've been learning a great deal about the power and moral authority of that.

I've learned from Barbara a tremendous amount about imaging, and about the whole cosmic sort of connection. And also the importance of the stress we all live with. We are, all three of us, trying to play midwife to evolutionary growth processes, and in so doing we subject ourselves to almost intolerable levels of stress. Barbara conveyed to me the idea that the stress was a part of the process, and that we weren't going to be able to learn to grow unless we could deal with the stress. I've been trying more and more to accept the stress. I've accepted the fact that the stress is going to be there until I die, because I'm doing what I ought to be doing. I'm throwing myself into the stream of the process—and it's okay.

Barbara: One thing that I learned last time was my very deep need for communion. We ended up being more moved by this communing that we had experienced together than by all of the intellectual debating. Each of us, I think, felt this deep need for contact and support at that level. And that was the value of that meeting over and above anything else. Whatever we do needs to have that dimension. If that isn't there, whatever it is, it won't be whole. It has to be whole person to whole person in any kind of interpersonal or organizational situation. I now understand that I cannot exercise my capacities without this dimension.

Because of this kind of whole-person-to-whole-person communing, Hazel and I, a year ago, were able to understand that the reason we have philosophical differences is that we have a different metaphysical view of reality.

Hazel: And different emotional themes.

Barbara: Yes! And a different temperamental attraction. But I think that we have learned to transcend that by sharing the pictures in our heads at the deepest possible level. We can then extend our pictures, and share the extended picture. Once we had realized that, and had seen the temperamental spectrum that we represent, and the ways in which our fathers had influenced those temperaments, we were able to laugh at all our arguments. Hazel can bring in an army of facts, and I can bring in an army of facts—

Hazel: But we've realized that those facts are just bullets in the information war that rationalize our own views.

Barbara: Our own passionate preferences! I have a passionate preference for the cosmos, and Hazel adores the Earth. But they are both realities!

Barbara DeLaney: Actually, on a higher level of integration, they're just aspects of one reality. And I think that that's one of the interesting things about many of your dialogues: that you've been able to communicate on a level where philosophical differences can be transcended. You succeed in expanding the focus to create the largest possible context—a context in which polarities become complementarities. And this again, I think, is an essential quality of what we've been calling yin thinking.

Hazel: Exactly!

Jean: Well, what I learned from our experience was the power of creative loving and of the mutual eliciting that takes place at that level of communality. It was something that had been missing from my life and work. In real communion there is a flow of being that is without the usual things that interrupt that flow. And this is something that—at least at this point in time—seems to be much more possible among women. I know that my own capacities are so much better when I am in that kind of state. Real communion is the time for the ending of personal charisma, of which I have too much and feel very bad about. In communion a field of force is set up in which healing, wholing, and growth become possible.

I am a member of many top-heavy, hierarchical organizations—many of which I sit on top of! To come into a situation in which there is so much love, so much sharing, listening and mutual eliciting—and laughter!—was probably the most democratizing experience of my life!

Barbara: That's right, Jean! You can be rather imperious! [laughter]

Jean: It's born and bred in me! But our experience allowed me to take all the people I work with—and step down. And empower them. And give them my position. Or at least a kind of implicit equality that they had never allowed me to give them before. I used to try, but only in a halfhearted way. I mean—do you realize that I've been president of the class since I was three years old? Do you know what that means? [laughter]

What happened, though, is that I found that other people's talents in my own organizations just began to bloom. I certainly owe that to our experience.

And another thing—something that happens here among us: We are looking so much at process that we are not looking at ends. We are living the means, the process, and not getting hung up on ends. And that's vital!

Hazel: Yes, what we are doing is trusting the interpersonal process. And it's a process that doesn't need or allow for hierarchies. This is something that is going to have to be learned. Take the marriage relationship, for instance. We even pretend that that is a hierarchical one, that it's a constant dominance/submission sort of interplay. If both parties would simply learn to trust the process of conflict resolution that they've developed, and to trust that their joint examination of the issues, and their joint decision making, is better than either one could have done individually! Why do we play this game?—that one is supposed to be dominant, and one is supposed to be submissive. It's a continual dance, and you have to learn to trust the process.

There are assumptions of hierarchy even in democracy that have to be examined. This relates to President Carter's current pain: the fact that he has to pretend to be the only one at the top, even though he's a sensible human being and knows that it's a consensual situation. But he's not able to get all the information he needs because there are too many bottlenecks. It's a continual charade! What this means is that the kind of new political movement that we are imaging has got to unfrock that game. We know that consensual decision making really goes on all the time—in government, in business . . . The head of a corporation doesn't really make all those decisions all by himself. This is the kind of understanding we need to explicate what is really going on in political process.

Barbara: Yes! In my Theater for the Future I show that if you look at creation—fifteen billion years of process, of which we, sitting here in this room, are the product—you know that it's inherent in the nature of reality that process can be trusted. If the nature of things were one percent more disintegrative than integrative, none of us would be here.

Jean: A lot of my snobbery about government, Hazel—dealing with the pterodactyls, as I used to call them—was wonderfully undermined by you when you talked about the humanizing of bureaucratic structures. I now have a completely different image. People in my field tend to be rather exclusive, particularly with respect to bureaucracies. You know: "Let's create something totally Other." Now what I've been able to do, and it's essentially from the inspiration I got from seeing how you operate, is to go into schools, hospitals, prisons, and get people to work within the existing process; to work within those bureaucracies. I've been learning your kind of strength of vision. And a kind of loving clarity—with anger. Before I never really had sufficient anger. I really learned that from you, Hazel; I've been learning a lot about creative intentionality in anger.

And from you, Barbara, I've learned the daring to be theological. I am basically a theological being, but I've kept my cards under the table; I've used other kinds of words. But I've learned from you to say the most wonderful, absurd things. I had always kept that part of me hidden. I find that in all my lectures now I am coming forward and talking about a much larger universe. For instance, I gave a theological address to the AMA recently—and they loved it! It's all up for grabs and we might as well say what we're really thinking!

Barbara: I think that that's what we've all been learning more and more.

Jean: I've also learned about suffering from Barbara. I find that a lot of my suffering had always been repressed because I didn't have the time for it. I feel very deep pain about some things, mostly having to do with other people's cruelties. I'm not quite as self-referential as you are, Barbara. I don't mean that in any egoistic way. You use yourself as the catalyst; whereas I tend to use event and process as the catalyst. But I am learning to use modes of personal pain to teach me, which I had not done before. It was very important for me to see that level of self-revelation. And now, in my work, there is much more real compassion. And also much more self-revealing, which I had never allowed before.

Barbara: Well, you know, I actually acted upon many of the things we had talked about last time. I got away for a while; I headed out to Findhorn. I reorganized my living situation. I withdrew from just about everything. It all had to do with this need *to die we had talked about last time. And I gave away cameras; I gave away the studio: I gave away a lot of that hardware. I started over again, basically on my own this time. I found that in getting rid of all the peripherals I was free to focus on the essentials of my own particular set of abilities, which means putting forward and activating a vision. And so in the last year I have poured my consciousness into the creation of the* Theater for the Future, *which I'm dying for you all to see. I've learned to focus on the uniqueness of my function. . . .*

And so on. An ongoing, transformative process. A deeply experienced mutuality in which everyone is acknowledged, challenged, mandated.

This has been, and continues to be, our experience together. It manifests in vital ways the growing edge of ourselves. We understand, as women have always understood, that growth is very much an interactive and mutually empowering process. This deep affiliative sensibility and sense of emotional/spiritual interdependence have always been central to female experience. Mutuality, trust, sharing, and love—secondary values relegated by historical circumstance to women—are indispensable requirements for the necessary planetary transformation. The influx of women into public spaces will most certainly infuse our political, social, and even corporate structures with a more holistic sensitivity to life—a healthy dose of *yin*! Hazel Henderson, Jean Houston, and Barbara Marx Hubbard, to name but three of many, are doing just that.

What began as a meeting of minds has evolved for us into a much deeper sharing of heart and spirit, something we have all come to treasure as a rich and nurturing source. A center. An evolutionary circle intersecting at many points with dynamic networks of women and men committed to activating New Age visions.

I myself, the silent presence and hopeful scribe of these pages, have perhaps reaped the richest treasures of all. Working with Jean Houston has taught me to attune myself not only to an expanded sense of mind-body potential, but also to a much larger sense of meaning and beingness. I have learned through Barbara Marx Hubbard to focus on the uniqueness of my own function, however that may evolve in the coming years. And I now dare to believe, thanks to Hazel Henderson, that I, too, am the bearer—as are we all—of a small bit of evolutionary potential. This experience has for me been a profound acknowledgement, an empowerment to accept the mandate of my own becoming.

Barbara DeLaney
1978

EPILOGUE

The following statements are taken from the
material taped on April 27, 1978.

Hazel Henderson

photo by Olan Mills

Until recently the goals of the industrial culture—the yang culture—had been very clear: to increase the GNP and those sorts of things. The premium was on action and the actors: the yang types who had all the power. But suddenly, as there is a crisis of nerve among the leaders, and it's not clear at all whether the goal actually *is* to maximize the GNP—there are signals coming from both the population and the planet itself that that doesn't really make sense anymore—the yang types are more or less left sitting there with their wheels spinning, waiting to engage the gears. At that point the people with the visions become absolutely essential. What I experience with the people in Washington that I deal with is that they are deferring right now to the vision makers.

This is why the political expression of our kinds of ideas, in whatever form it may take, will be very largely populated by women: simply because we have been historically relegated to being the intuitives, the visionaries, and to expressing that part of ourselves. I have been trying to map how many decision centers in the system are being programmed by charismatic, visionary women— or poets and other male or female yin types. We should expect to find those sorts of people having enormous moral authority.

Jean Houston

photo by Christopher Briscoe

The image of Woman had hitherto been a carryover from Neolithic days, where she was a symbol of fecundity, birth, and so on. I think that the rise of the feminine archetype is of a very different order now: It is Woman as a principle of creative transformation. We are saying, "Ladies and gentlemen, this is not working! Let us find the new visions; let us find the new economics; let us find the ecology to make it work!" It's the end of dialectic, the end of polarity. It's an entirely different thing. We are responding to the sheer absurdity of things. And we are the only ones who can say that the emperor has no clothes!

I've been looking at the way this image is rising in a great many people. It isn't the old Mother Goddess anymore. What is coming from the depths is a highly energized, very brilliant, very innovative, and rather comical female figure. The sense of irony, the sense of the comic, are very strong.

Part of the creative transformation is investment. The fact is, *we* are not vested in the past. Our investment is in the future.

Barbara Marx Hubbard

photo by Glenn Derbyshire

My choice of acts in response to the revived sense of urgency I've experienced in the last year was to put together a multimedia presentation for my *Theater for the Future* that I've called *Previews of Coming Attractions*. It's essentially a creation story—fifteen billion years of process—and we are all participants in the creation. This last loop on the evolutionary spiral, our design innovation comparable to photosynthesis, or the genetic code, or culture, is conscious evolution. We need to understand the process, and attune ourselves to it. In my presentation I lay out what it might be like if it works. Someone has to dare to say, "It might be this great!" I'm imaging a healthy planet. I'm imaging what it might be like if everything works. It's so joyful, so irresistible. Just as we know all the pieces of the breakdown, we basically know the pieces of the breakthrough.

Barbara DeLaney

photo by Sylvie Lucien

The female principle is beginning to capture the collective imagination and to quicken all sorts of new possibilities. I've been experiencing among groups of very different types of women a dynamism—a new sense of sorority. And that tends to make men very uneasy, but only because they don't yet understand what that might mean, quite positively, for them.

NOTES

page 35:
1. *Small Is Beautiful,* by E. F. Schumacher (Harper & Row, 1973)

page 43:
2. *The Tao of Physics,* by Fritjof Capra (Shambhala Publications, 1975)

page 84:
3. *Cosmic Consciousness,* by R.M. Bucke (1901)

page 95:
4. *The Great Transformation,* by Karl Polanyi (Beacon Press, 1944)

page 96:
5. *The Hunger of Eve: A Woman's Odyssey Toward the Future,* by Barbara Marx Hubbard (Stackpole, 1976)

page 108:
6. *Prolongevity,* by Albert Rosenfeld (Knopf, 1976)

page 109:
7. *Listening to the Body: The Psychophysical Way to Health,* by Robert Masters and Jean Houston (Delacorte Press, 1978)

page 115:
8. *A Course in Miracles,* by Foundation for Inner Peace (1975)

page 150:
9. *The Lives of a Cell,* by Lewis Thomas (The Viking Press, 1974)

COSIMO is a specialty publisher of books and publications that inspire, inform, and engage readers. Our mission is to offer unique books to niche audiences around the world.

COSIMO BOOKS publishes books and publications for innovative authors, nonprofit organizations, and businesses. **COSIMO BOOKS** specializes in bringing books back into print, publishing new books quickly and effectively, and making these publications available to readers around the world.

COSIMO CLASSICS offers a collection of distinctive titles by the great authors and thinkers throughout the ages. At **COSIMO CLASSICS** timeless works find new life as affordable books, covering a variety of subjects including: Business, Economics, History, Personal Development, Philosophy, Religion & Spirituality, and much more!

COSIMO REPORTS publishes public reports that affect your world, from global trends to the economy, and from health to geopolitics.

FOR MORE INFORMATION CONTACT US AT
INFO@COSIMOBOOKS.COM

❋ if you are a book lover interested in our current catalog of books

❋ if you represent a bookstore, book club, or anyone else interested in special discounts for bulk purchases

❋ if you are an author who wants to get published

❋ if you represent an organization or business seeking to publish books and other publications for your members, donors, or customers.

**COSIMO BOOKS ARE ALWAYS
AVAILABLE AT ONLINE BOOKSTORES**

**VISIT COSIMOBOOKS.COM
BE INSPIRED, BE INFORMED**

Printed in the United States
88429LV00003B/52-123/A

9 781596 058873